Pathway to the Spirit World

A True Account of a Near-Death Experience

Pathway to the Spirit World

by

Hashi-Hanta

A Book for All People

FIRST AMERICAN PUBLISHING ● PASADENA, CALIFORNIA

First American Publishing
Suite 514
30 North Raymond Avenue
Pasadena, California 91103

©1995 by Hashi-Hanta

Cover Design–Lightbourne Images, Original Art–Jesse Bilyeu

ISBN: 0-9645421-5-3

Library of Congress Card Catalog Number: 95-060303

First American Publishing hardcover printing June 1995

10 9 8 7 6 5 4 3 2 1

Printed in the United States of America

For information, or additional copies of this book if unavailable in local bookstores, contact First American Publishing, 30 North Raymond Avenue, Suite 514, Pasadena, CA 91103, (818) 798-7298 or fax (818) 798-7398.

This book is dedicated with love to

my husband, Rupert, who is the
quiet strength behind my achievements

my sons, Pete and Na Humma,
who bring the greatest joy to my life

and my beloved brother, Mike,
who is now in the Spirit World.

CONTENTS

CONTENTS

PREFACE

*B*efore my accident I feared death. Afterward, when the pain was unbearable, I longed for death. I then died, traveled to the Spirit World, returned to Earth, and found I was free of either fear or longing.

Death should not be feared—death is merely a transition into another realm. When we accept death as a natural part of life, we gain the freedom to fully enjoy our time here on Earth.

In order for our lives to be complete, we must have both purpose and pleasure. We have a responsibility to help heal both our civilization and Earth. We also have the right to lead a full, happy, and successful life. Poverty, pain, and suffering are not required to be a good person. We have the right to pursue a lifestyle of our choosing.

When we are spiritually sound, good things naturally come our way. Not only are we at peace with ourselves and our surroundings, but our goals in life also appear to take a clearer direction.

While I was in the Spirit World, I learned many things that are important to all people. Although I am a Choctaw woman, the things I was shown are for individuals of all races and cultures.

In Native American nations, we usually refer to God as "Creator," "Grandfather," "Great Mystery," or "Great Spirit."

In an attempt to make this book understood by all readers, I have referred to our Creator as "God" or "Creator." There is one God, and when we pray from our hearts by whatever name we call Him, our prayers are heard.

This book is written as a guide to help people find their own spiritual path. Like traditional Native American teaching, it tells a story—a true account of my life and death. When I traveled to the Spirit World, Creator shared with me His Original Instructions. I would now like to share these instructions with you.

Hashi-Hanta
June 1995

ACKNOWLEDGMENTS

I would like to sincerely thank all those who have given me both love and help on my earthly journey, as well as those who contributed so greatly to making this book a reality.

Many, many thanks to my cousin, Jennifer, for a lifetime of unconditional love, of which often I was unworthy; to the memory of Jessie and Paul Carmichael, "Mama" and "Daddy," Vera Jacobs Hoyle, "GoGo," and Nell Garfield Snedden, "Mama Big," for never ceasing to love and support a very difficult child; to my brother, Steve, whose brilliance and achievements fill me with sisterly pride; to the memory of Mad Bear, respected friend, elder and spiritual advisor who truly understood my journey to the Spirit World; to Charline Abernathy and Anthea Cappas for always being in my corner and providing shelter from the storm; to my dear friend, Toni Lone Hawk, for her never-ending support and encouragement, and for the food we shared during our very broke days; to Linda and Bob Appel who saved my life by putting themselves at risk to bring me out of Mexico; to Mike Reed who cared for me when I was unable to care for myself; to Sam and Sheldon Allman, my dear, dear friends who have all the answers to my endless and oftentimes difficult questions; to Cristina whose loving and highly skilled care of Na Humma enabled my work to continue; to Gaelyn Larrick, Lightbourne Images, whose expert help and guidance created the cover for this book and much more; to Jesse Bilyeu for his patience during all my changes to his fabulous artwork; to Sharon Goldinger, PeopleSpeak, for her skillful and tireless editing and for her acceptance when I refused to follow the rules; to Dale Schroeder, Synergistic Data Systems, for his design expertise, which helped us to finally pull it all together; to Dan Poynter whose vast knowledge of publishing enabled me to get this book off my computer; and last, but not least, to my four-legged and winged family members—Bud, Foo Foo I, Foo Foo II, Ha-Soe, Omar, Chum Boy, Nooley, Tout-Sweet and Cat Ballou—who through the years have brought unreserved love and joy to my life.

*I am an aged tree, and can stand no longer
. . . I go to join the spirits of my fathers,
where age cannot come.*

—Red Jacket, Seneca, 1830

CHAPTER ONE

A Change of Worlds

There is no death, only a change of worlds.

—Seathl, Dwamish chief, 1854

I could hear doctors' voices. I knew they were talking about me, but it didn't seem to matter. I didn't have the strength to open my eyes. I was amazed that I was even alive. I had traveled to the Spirit World, stood before Creator, and now I had returned. The doctors' voices continued.

"She was gone for almost five minutes."

"She'll be a vegetable."

"She'll never make it."

"It's too bad. She's only twenty-six. I'll bet she was really pretty."

"A *pretty Indian?*"

"I'll bet she was a *beautiful* Indian."

I thought about my young son. I wanted to live so that I could care for him, but I was not sure that was possible. I felt that at any moment I could die again and this time I might not be allowed to return.

The doctors' voices interrupted my thoughts. "We've got to get that blood off. It's too much pressure." Then they began to discuss a baseball game. I couldn't believe it—I was lying there, dying, and these supposedly caring physicians were discussing baseball.

The blood that the doctors were referring to was the blood that had accumulated beneath the right side of my face. Two days earlier I had been in a near-fatal automobile accident. My back and neck were broken. A big chunk of flesh was torn off of my right shin, exposing the bone. My jaw had numerous fractures and was completely broken at the chin. My right cheek was crushed. The dark glasses I had been wearing had gone through my cheek. My right eye had been turned around in the socket. The right side of my face and head was filled with blood and horribly, grossly extended outward. I looked like something out of a horror movie.

The doctors were now operating, trying to remove the blood from around my brain, save my right eye, and wire my shattered facial bones together. They inserted tubes into my face, which remained there for several days, draining off blood.

As the doctors were finishing, I kept drifting in and out of consciousness. Finally, the room became very quiet and I assumed that everyone had left. I managed to barely open my eyes and saw a very attractive doctor looking down at me.

"You're going to be all right," he assured me. "Your face will be just fine. You know when you're better, I'd really like to see you."

"What?" I was sure I had misunderstood him.

"I'd like to go out with you," he said, smiling, as he squeezed my hand.

"I look hideous," I groaned.

"You'll be fine in no time, and I'd really like to see you," he insisted.

"Okay, sure," I murmured.

"Oh, you say that now, but you'll forget me once you're out of the hospital," he said, still holding my hand.

"No, no, I'll remember," I managed to say before losing consciousness.

I regained consciousness a few minutes later as I was being wheeled down a hospital corridor. I felt like I was living a nightmare. The doctors here discussed baseball while operating, and a doctor, who had to be either blind or extremely kinky, had asked me out. I knew I had to get out of this hospital and into another, but I had no strength to do anything, much less change hospitals. I was only able to remain conscious for a minute or two, and I still wasn't convinced I would even live.

When I came to again, I was in a hospital bed and a nurse was jabbing away at my arm with a needle. I guess she finally found a vein because all of a sudden blood started spurting out onto the sheets and even onto the wall near the bed. I had lived through an incredible accident, managed to stay alive against unbelievable odds, died, and returned to Earth, and now this nurse was going to let me bleed to death. Mercifully, I again lost consciousness.

When I next opened my eyes, I saw that my blood was still on both the sheets and the wall. So much for cleanliness. I wondered if anyone else was in the room. I was so weak I could only move my eyes. My entire world consisted of the hospital bed and the area immediately surrounding it. I cannot begin to describe the extent of the pain I was experiencing. I wanted to ring or call for a nurse, but I was too weak to move. Somewhere in the distance I could hear someone yelling—horrible, tormented screams. It sounded as if the person were being tortured. Nothing else could produce such cries of agony. Then I realized that the screams were my own—I had no control over them. I couldn't even feel them coming from my throat, but what I could feel was pain. If it had not been for my son, I would have gladly died.

As young as I was, I had already lived a pretty full life. I had experienced more in twenty-six years than most people do in a lifetime. Since I had lived in Hollywood I had been politically active in Native American issues and also had friends in the music world (as well as complimentary passes to the clubs and rock concerts). I went to parties given by top rock groups in Beverly Hills and Bel Air. I was a guest, not a groupie. I had dated men from Elvis Presley to the world famous matador, El Cordobés. Life had been fun.

But my son was my *real* reason for living. He was my life and I couldn't leave him. I wanted to be sure he would never be in need, that he would be safe and secure, and that his life would be happy. I understood that every minute I lived was a gift from Creator. He had allowed me to come back to finish my work here on Earth. I believed He must have plans for me or I wouldn't be alive. I felt if only I could be strong enough to live, a meaningful life would be waiting.

CHAPTER TWO

A New Life

*There is no evil in my heart. My song is the
song of peace.*

—Kiosaton, Iroquois chief, 1645

$\mathcal{M}$y time spent in the hospital was truly one of the worst experiences of my life—each day seemed an eternity. I wish I could have looked into the future and seen the positive changes that would soon take place in my life.

After I returned from the Spirit World and recovered from my injuries, my life changed dramatically. I had always cared about animals and the Earth, and I had never intentionally tried to hurt anyone. If I was asked for help, I did the best I could to provide it. I now realize that my past efforts were not enough.

In the Spirit World I had been shown many things including important information that I now had to share with whoever would listen. But I also wanted people to understand that even though I had been somewhere that most

7

people have not yet gone, I was really no different from anyone else.

Anyone who really wants to can turn his or her life around. Life is what we choose to make it. Love, happiness, and success are possible if we know the right way to achieve them.

By telling the story of my life, I hope people will understand that if *I* was able to make positive changes, *anyone* can. You don't have to walk on eggshells or be a "goodie two shoes" to be spiritual. You simply have to bring God into your daily life and take some responsibility for the future of our world.

When I traveled to the Spirit World, I was able to look back at Earth. I had clearly seen the end of our civilization. The planet was nothing but a barren wasteland. I knew I had to do as much as I could to prevent this total destruction. I wanted to know that my son and his children would be able to enjoy the beautiful Earth that Creator entrusted to our care.

Even with all of the disabilities I suffered from my auto accident, I felt stronger than ever before. I knew who I was. Parties and nightclubs no longer held any interest. Although I had never had a drinking problem, I used to love my margaritas. Now the thought of more than one or two drinks a year was unpleasant. I felt that I no longer needed acceptance from the outside world—what I needed was already inside of me.

On a personal level, my life began to change. The change was gradual but with absolute direction. One of my first pursuits was to apply for certification as a member of the Choctaw Nation. The government had cut off our formal rolls long before I was born, so I was forced to apply to the Bureau of Indian Affairs. I felt it a rather degrading experience having to turn to the United States government for proof of my identity, but I seemed to have no other choice.

Fourteen months after my accident, with the help of a tribal scholarship, I enrolled at the University of California at Los Angeles (UCLA) and later graduated with a degree in political science. After graduation, I worked for Metromedia as a radio newsperson and a radio and television talk show host.

After leaving radio and television, I started my own real estate investment firm and moved into the top 20 percent of female wage earners in the country. I have lectured to thousands of people on successful investment methods, but in every lecture I also mention the critical need to save our environment.

For many years one of my greatest wishes was to have another child. However, after years of struggling as a single parent, I knew that before I brought another life into the world I should first have a strong marriage. Since I had returned from the Spirit World, I could clearly see the need for two loving parents to properly raise a child. Therefore, if I was to fulfill my dream of having another baby, I would first have to find a husband. This would be no easy task.

Today, the Native American population in the United States is approximately two million. The census rolls show that more than one-half of that population is under twenty years of age. Of those over twenty, at least half are women. Of the fewer than 500,000 men left, many are married and some are elderly. Others, for various reasons, are not eligible for marriage.

I meet women every day who would like to be married or at least be in a meaningful relationship. The usual complaint I hear is "A good man is hard to find." I agree, and for Native American women who are no longer under twenty-five, it's almost impossible.

In 1986, I met, and seven months later married, a young, handsome, intelligent, caring Native American man who today is a wonderful husband and father. Considering my age then and the lack of eligible men, I thought this was somewhat of a miracle. An even greater miracle was the fact that this very eligible man was interested in me. We were married in a traditional ceremony by Grandfather White Cloud, a Native American elder. Our marriage was blessed with a son who gives us endless joy. When my older son graduated from college, he was academically in the top one-half of one percent of all college students in the country. I thank God every day for my wonderful life.

Shortly before I met my husband, the real estate market in California began to experience a serious downfall. When we were married, he not only made a commitment to share his life with me and my two elderly cats, but he also accepted the fact that I had a failing real estate investment business that was making me slightly crazy.

Although, as of the writing of this book, the California real estate market is still in a slump, my husband and I have rebuilt our business. Working together and adapting to the current market, we have made our business more successful than ever before.

Success is not a sin. If we live each day to the best of our ability, acting in a spiritually responsible manner, we deserve a full and happy life. We each have many God-given rights: to succeed and achieve one's goals; to pursue happiness; to have a rewarding career; to obtain financial independence for ourselves and our families; to have good doctors and dentists; and to enjoy fulfilling relationships with our spouse or lover, our children, our parents, our extended family, our friends and acquaintances. God brings happiness into our lives. We create our own unhappiness.

I believe that through sincere prayer and an earnest attempt to follow the instructions shown to me by Creator, I have become spiritually, emotionally, and financially sound. I believe that each of us is entitled to joy and security in life. Creator did not put us on Earth to suffer—neither did he put us on Earth to make others suffer.

We were given a paradise in which to live, but we have systematically attempted to destroy it. We must work to reclaim that lost paradise, both emotionally and environmentally. If we are not spiritually strong, we will never know true happiness. A spiritually strong person can accept happiness without guilt. A full and happy life frees us from worry and allows us to use our time to work harder in the service of others.

We hold the key to bringing change into our lives. We control our future. If we believe in ourselves and act on those beliefs, we can have a lifestyle of our own choosing. We deserve to have happiness. We deserve to have success. We deserve to have security. We deserve to have love.

Through the power of prayer, we will find spiritual guidance and bring God into our lives. With our spirituality intact, we will have better personal relationships, more successful business ventures, and much less stress. We will move toward greater health and prosperity, and we will truly be reborn into the love and protection of God. With our spiritual power in place, we will be able to choose the right direction for our lives.

We are created by God and therefore are capable of great things. Through prayer or meditation, we open our minds to the wisdom of the ages. These age-old truths can lead us toward a better self, a better life, and a better world.

When we learn to no longer fear death, we experience a rebirth. Fear is removed from our lives and we are free to enjoy a glorious life here on Earth. We live each day to the fullest. We discover a joy we never before knew possible. Everything we do takes on a new meaning. We know that death is not an end to life. One day, we will simply leave one world to transcend into another.

CHAPTER THREE

The Flower of Friendship

*Like a brilliant quetzal plume, a fragrant
blooming flower, friendship sparkles and
dances.*

—Aztec poem of friendship

I lay in the hospital bed drifting in and out of consciousness. I knew I was in Los Angeles and that the hospital I was in was not a good one. There would be little care here. If I was to live, it was up to me and Creator.

I was thankful to still be alive, yet I prayed for strength to bear the pain. Headaches are painful—migraines, if bad enough, can put you in a hospital. No words can describe what a critical head injury feels like. A nurse came in every few hours and gave me a shot, but it did nothing for the pain. It was like throwing a cup of water on a forest fire.

I tried to think back to the accident, but my memory only came back in bits and pieces. Even now, twenty-five years later, I can't completely remember the accident itself.

My girlfriend, Linda, and I were in Mexico for the weekend. I was seeing a young bullfighter and had convinced

Linda that she should come along for the adventure. As we were walking through our hotel lobby on Sunday morning, we ran into Miguel, a friend from Los Angeles. We had all been out dancing the night before and had returned to the hotel quite late. Miguel said that he was going to Plaza Monumental with some friends and asked if we wanted to go. We accepted his invitation.

When we reached the car, we learned that six of us would be going. Fortunately, Miguel's girlfriend, Jackie, had decided not to go. Miguel said she had started to get dressed but then changed her mind at the last minute. This was unusual for Jackie who was young and pretty, loved a good time, and seldom turned down an invitation to go anywhere. I'm sure that her last minute decision not to go with Miguel that morning probably saved her life.

Linda and I got into the backseat with Miguel and another man. Even though the car was large, it was crowded in the backseat with Linda and me sitting between the two men. The man driving and another man were in the bucket seats in the front. If Jackie had been with us, Miguel would probably have been sitting in the front seat with Jackie on his lap. In an accident, she very likely would have gone through the windshield.

We were at the plaza for less than an hour, and at about 12:45 P.M. we started back to the hotel. The road leading through the mountains and back into town was new and well-paved. It was a clear, sunny day and traffic was not heavy. We had been on the road only two or three minutes when I realized we were traveling at a very high speed. I whispered to Linda, "This guy's going too fast. I'm going to tell him to slow down or we'll get out and get a taxi." At the exact moment that I started to lean forward to talk to the driver, he missed the turn that headed back into town. He swerved drastically, still trying to make the turn, and by doing so, threw the car over the cliff.

The next thing I remember, I was being pushed down a hall in a wheelchair. I remember trying to talk to the young man that was pushing me. I felt myself losing consciousness and was sure I was dying.

When I regained consciousness, I was lying on a mattress covered by a dirty sheet and Linda was sitting beside me. Since the whole weekend had been my idea, I was grateful that I was the one who was critically injured and not Linda. She kept telling me to hang on, that she was going to get me back into California and everything would be all right. She said that the doctor had sent someone to a drug store to get something to turn my eye back around. I had no idea what she was talking about, but I somehow knew that my face had been destroyed. I made Linda promise not to let anyone know where I was because I didn't want to be seen looking like I did. Linda's voice sounded very faraway and then everything went black again.

Linda later told me that the doctor stitched up two huge gashes on my right check and used some kind of a plastic stick to turn my right eye back around in the socket. They didn't have any anesthetic; they just held me down. She said my screams were horrifying. Mercifully, I don't remember any of it.

When I awakened again, Linda was still sitting beside me. She said she was trying to get a phone call through to the States, to her boyfriend, Bob, so that he could come and get us. I prayed that call would go through soon.

I heard Linda asking the elderly woman in the next bed if she knew where we could get a blanket and pillow. The woman answered in English, "Honey, we're very poor. We don't have any blankets or pillows." I prayed harder for Bob to come for us.

I don't remember regaining consciousness again for over twenty-four hours. Then I was sitting up in the backseat of a car. It was dark, but I could see the bright border crossing lights through the windshield. Linda was sitting in the front seat and Bob was behind the steering wheel talking to the border guard. I heard him say, "We're all Americans." The guard smiled and waved us through. I was amazed. Usually all passengers in the car have to individually state their citizenship and since many people have never seen a Native American, I am many times mistaken for a Mexican. I also couldn't understand why the guard didn't ask about my very obvious injuries. I said a short prayer of thanks before blacking out again.

Linda worked for a doctor in Anaheim, which was about an hour away from where I lived in Los Angeles. The hospital where he sent his patients was supposed to be one of the best in the county—this is where Bob took us. Linda was examined, diagnosed as having a concussion, told to go home to bed, and then released. They left me at the hospital, assuming that at such a fine hospital, I would be well taken care of. They were wrong.

While we were still in Mexico, besides calling Bob, Linda had also called a good friend of mine, Mike, to see if he could help us. Mike was a young African American man who was involved in the entertainment industry and had also just opened a bail bond business. His answering service had not been able to locate him, but Linda left a message explaining our situation. When Mike got the message, he drove to Tijuana and went to all of the hospitals trying to find us. Unable to locate us, he started back to California, using his car phone to stay in touch with his answering service and calling Linda's apartment over and over.

It was after midnight and he was back in Los Angeles before Linda finally answered. She told him that when people are injured in an auto accident in Mexico, it is against Mexican law to let them out of the country. Bob actually had to bribe a doctor to tell the hospital that he was taking Linda and me to another hospital in Tijuana before we were finally released. He and Linda then washed the blood from my face, propped me up in the backseat of the car, and headed for the border. Bob was about twelve years older than Linda and I, professional, and very levelheaded. He said he never believed I'd live to reach the hospital in Anaheim.

I opened my eyes as I felt strong arms gently picking me up. I looked up into Mike's concerned, caring face and for the first time since the accident, I felt safe. Since I didn't have medical insurance and the hospital refused to take Mike's check in the middle of the night, Mike had no choice but to risk my life further by taking me in his car to Los Angeles. The hospital in Anaheim wouldn't even let Mike use a wheelchair or gurney to take me out to the parking lot. Mike had a friend with him who sat in the backseat holding me until we reached Los Angeles. Without insurance, I still couldn't get into a private hospital, so Mike had to leave me in the county hospital, where, within a few hours, I was to die.

I thank God for friends like Linda and Mike; without them, I would never have made it to Los Angeles. Linda and I had been good friends since the fifth grade, and although I had only known Mike two years we had become very close. Nothing is as meaningful as true friends.

CHAPTER FOUR

Days of Joy—Nights of Terror

*Man and wife should rear their children
well, love them and keep them in health.*

—Handsome Lake, early 1800s

I was raised by my grandparents in Santa Ana, California. At that time it was a nice medium-sized town, with two junior high schools and one senior high. There was little crime, at least not enough to cause concern. There were no gangs or drugs. Life for most people was fairly simple.

We lived on the north side of town, which was considered the "better side." It was not a situation where there was a "right" or a "wrong" side of town—the north side simply had more expensive houses and was considered "better." The most expensive houses were on the northeast side of town. We lived on the northwest.

Until I started kindergarten, my life was pretty uneventful. In my mind, my grandparents were my parents. My grandmother was only thirty-nine when I was born and she looked at least ten years younger. I called them "Mama" and "Daddy" and our loving household was happy and orderly, which gave me a sense of security. I knew I had a mother, but she lived in Los Angeles and only visited us for a few hours on Saturdays or Sundays. I believed my father was dead. I had been told that he had "gone to war and never come back." Well, that was true in a sense. He had gone overseas with the military and he never did come back—at least not to us. I would later find out that he was alive, healthy, successful, and living in Oklahoma.

We lived in a Cape Cod-style house on a tree-lined street. My grandfather worked very hard to support us and even though he never made a large salary, my grandmother was great at managing money. But I was acutely aware that it was a financial struggle to maintain our comfortable lifestyle. We never received a penny of support from either my father or my mother.

As soon as I was an adult and had children they became my reason for living. I cannot understand how parents could give up their children. I guess if I were in a situation where I couldn't even feed them, out of love, I might give them to a family that could take better care of them—but that would be the only reason. If getting a divorce meant giving up my children, I would live with Dracula himself before I would let them go. I thank God every day that I was raised by my adoring grandparents who provided such a wonderful home for me and gave me the freedom to find myself.

Outside of my grandparents, two other people were very important in my childhood. Probably the most important person in my life, who instilled in me a sense of fairness and decent values, was my grandmother's sister. Her name was Vera, but all the kids called her "GoGo." She truly loved children but had never been able to have any of her own. She seemed to know that my life would not be easy. From the time I was born and for the rest of her life, she spent every day trying to make sure I was happy and prepared for life's hardships. She also spoiled me terribly. If I wanted a new toy or if I asked her to get down on the floor and play with me, she never said no. She always told me how beautiful and brilliant and wonderful I was. Looking back, I know she did her best to make me as self-confident as possible. She knew that soon I would be a little Native American girl in an all-white school in a very conservative town, and I would need all the help I could get.

The other person who was, and still is, extremely important to me is my cousin, Jennifer. She is seven months older than I, and although we are not first or even second cousins, we saw each other almost every day of our lives until we were grown. Actually, we are much more like sisters than cousins.

Jennifer was the sweetest child who ever lived. She never did anything wrong, was kind and loving, and always tried to help people in any way that she could. On the other hand, I was an absolute terror. When I did something wrong, which was quite often, everyone (except GoGo) would say, "Why can't you act like Jennifer?" As much as I loved Jennifer and wanted to play with her every day, I also had feelings of resentment and jealousy that I didn't understand.

Jennifer was thin and had blond curly hair, she had two "real" parents, and she took tap dancing. In my pre-schooler's mind, this was as perfect as a little girl could be. I was the complete opposite. I was short and sturdy with olive skin and long, thick black braids. Jennifer looked like the other little girls in our town. I did not.

Jennifer's parents, Winnie and Willard, would take us on picnics where I would do my best to behave and not make them mad at me. Winnie used to take a big, red plaid, metal cooler filled with Delaware Punch to those picnics. I thought that cooler was the greatest thing I had ever seen. To me, it was a symbol of the all-American family.

Jennifer and I played together almost daily. I was always glad to see her, but for some reason, every day before she went home, I had to beat her up. She would come back the next day and say, "Let's not fight today." I'd say, "Okay, let's just pretend we're fighting," and then I'd beat her up again. But no matter how mean I was to her, no matter how many times I fought with her, she kept coming back, and she never stopped loving me. To this day, I would trust her with my life.

I also played with the children who lived on my street. Living next door to us was Colleen, a beautiful little girl who was six months older than I. She was half-French and half-Irish and had black hair, blue eyes, and fair skin with freckles across her nose. I think we started playing together before we could even walk. We usually played dolls or mud pies and we called each other "Mrs. Smeeker." I have no idea where we got that name, but we did that up until the time we started school.

When Colleen was about three years old, she started going to nursery school in the mornings. I couldn't wait for her to come home every afternoon so we could play. There were other little girls on the street, but they were older, and no one had as much fun as Colleen and I.

Somehow, before each afternoon ended, we would manage to get into a terrible argument. Colleen would stand on her front lawn and I would stand on my driveway. We stood there, nose to nose, and dared each other to step over the line onto the other's property.

We made tents around our big sycamore tree. If it was raining, we made tents with blankets draped over chairs in our den. My grandmother was an immaculate housekeeper, but we were always free to play in our den or my bedroom. We'd eat popcorn, have toys spread out, and then at four o'clock, Colleen would go home and my grandmother would pick up after us.

Before dinner, my grandmother always gave me a bath, put a clean dress on me, and rebraided my hair. I miss those days when every night I sat down at our dinner table and enjoyed a delicious, well-balanced, home-cooked meal.

My preschool days were wonderful, but the nights were very different. I was terrified of the dark. I always slept with my bedroom door open and the hall light on. And then there were the dreams. I had many different nightmares that I no longer remember, but one that I had almost nightly is as clear in my mind today as it was all those years ago.

This dream is especially important because it shows how closely my relatives who lived before me were watching over me. They were trying to warn me of the dangers that lay ahead, but I was simply too young to understand.

The dream was always the same and took place in the backyard at GoGo's house. She and her husband, Uncle Bud, and my great-grandmother, whom we called "Mama Big," lived about four blocks from us. They had a beautiful, two-story house that they had designed and built shortly before I was born. It was white with green shutters, just like our house. And like our house, it had a brick walk that went up to the brick front porch. I loved their house. It was immaculately clean and the refrigerator was always filled with food. No one could cook like Mama Big. She made pies with the flakiest crusts imaginable and mouth-watering cakes, too; every Monday, she baked bread and rolls. I used to love walking up the driveway on Monday mornings, passing the kitchen window, and smelling the bread as it baked. I couldn't wait for it to be finished so that I could have a slice while it was still warm and cover it with real butter. (At our house, we only had margarine, but I had dreams of being rich when I grew up and always having real butter.)

Although my grandparents' house was well-run and very clean, and we had wonderful meals every night, I knew how carefully my grandmother watched our money to make ends meet. At GoGo's house there always appeared to be plenty of money. She and Uncle Bud were careful with their money—he was more careful than anyone I've ever seen—but they could always buy anything they wanted. Anytime I wanted money, it was never refused. If GoGo bought clothes for herself, she also bought something for my grand-mother. The two sisters were very close and GoGo was completely unselfish. GoGo bought all of my clothes and most of my toys.

Since GoGo's house was the epitome of my safety and security, I think it was an important message that my worst nightmare always placed me in her backyard. In my dream, GoGo and my grandmother were lying out in the sun on the lawn. I started to walk toward them when suddenly men appeared. They came walking through the six-foot-tall, white picket fence that surrounded the backyard. (They somehow were able to walk right through the fence boards.) The men were identical and in a never-ending line. They wore white uniforms and hats, similar to what a house painter would wear. The only skin that was visible, on their faces, necks, and hands, was covered with what appeared to be white paint. They marched in military fashion, swinging their arms back and forth. Their backs were stiff and their faces were looking straight ahead. Although they had eyes and ears, they could not see or hear. I knew they were coming after me.

I screamed and ran back toward the house. Although GoGo and my grandmother were just a few feet away, they couldn't hear my screams. The men marched right past them, but Mama and GoGo didn't even know they were there, much less that they were after me. There was no way that they, or anyone else, could stop them.

Before I reached the porch that ran across the back of GoGo's house, I saw a doghouse. (I'm not sure why this was in the dream—GoGo never had a dog or doghouse in her backyard.) When I saw the doghouse, I thought I would be safe inside. I knew that animals were my friends, and if there was a dog inside it would protect me.

When I crawled inside the doghouse, there were spider webs on the ceiling ready to drop and entrap me. I knew then that there was no escape. These men, who were completely white and could neither see nor hear, were going to get me. No one could save me; only I could save myself.

At that point I always awoke from the nightmare. I tried to scream for my grandmother, but I was so terrified, I had no voice. I must have been screaming in my sleep though because when I awakened, Mama was always standing beside my crib. She would pick me up and hold me until I fell asleep again.

I dreaded going to sleep at night for fear the nightmare would return. To this day, although I no longer have nightmares, I still fight sleep every night.

When I was in grade school, I began to have another nightmare. I dreamed I was being chased by a crowd of people in Santa Ana who were trying to hurt me. I ran as fast as I could and just when their arms reached out to grab me, I would begin to fly. It was almost as if I were running through the air but high enough to be just out of reach of their fingertips.

I could feel their hands right below my feet. I was very tired and it was hard to keep going, but I knew I had to get away from them. I seemed to understand that if I tried hard enough, I would be able to stay above those who had so much hatred in their hearts.

I stopped having nightmares about the men in white before I reached my teens. However, the nightmare of flying above a hostile crowd continued until I was twenty-four and moved away from Orange County, California.

CHAPTER FIVE

Seeking Acceptance

The Great Spirit made all men brothers . . .
It is not the color of the skin that makes me
good or bad.

—White Shield, Arikara chief, 1867

Elementary school was an extremely painful experience. The first day of kindergarten was terrifying. My grandmother walked with me to my classroom, introduced me to my teacher, Mrs. Tedrow, and then left. I felt as if my whole world were leaving with her.

I found a chair and sat down. The other children were laughing, talking, and busy making new friends. As I sat in my chair, I looked around the room at all the wonderful toys. I especially liked the brightly painted wooden blocks. They were about two feet square, and some children were making a tunnel out of them and then crawling through. I wanted desperately to go over and play with those beautiful blocks, but I was too frightened to move.

Kindergarten through third grade were horrible. I tried to make the best of things by being as quiet as possible and hoping that none of the other children would even notice me. I still have my first grade report card. My teacher wrote on it, "She's just like a little owl. She's so quiet. She won't say anything unless called upon." It was a very sad time of my life.

One little boy was especially mean to me. He was a sturdily built little boy with white-blond hair and a vicious disposition— a real bully. One day I climbed up the ladder to the monkey bars. He was right above me on the ladder and when he looked down and saw me, he kicked me very hard with the heel of his oxfords. His shoe hit me right below my lower lip. The pain made me dizzy, and I could feel a warm stream of blood running down my chin. I ran crying to Mrs. Tedrow and she took me to the school nurse. I still have the scar.

In kindergarten, we sometimes worked with clay and made animal figures. I always made four figures: a father, mother, and two babies. Then I would wrap them together very tightly so they would always be close together and no one would ever be lonely.

Grade school was a very, very lonely place for me. The children in my class seemed to take special delight in pointing out that my parents had dumped me and I had to live with my grandparents. Hardly a day passed that someone didn't ask why my parents gave me away. I had no answer. I was further ostracized because my parents were divorced. I tried to explain that the marriage had actually been annulled, but it made no difference. At that time in Orange County, a divorced person was only slightly more popular than a communist or a leper.

Occasionally, one of the little girls would invite me to go home with her after school. I always accepted, thinking that now I might have a friend. However, the next day, the child would always say, "My mother wants to know what you are. You're Mexican, aren't you? My mother says I can't play with you anymore."

After two or three of the girls took me home, no one ever asked again. I tried to explain that I was Native American, but that didn't seem to make any difference. Most people think that prejudice is rampant in the South. They obviously have never been in Orange County.

In elementary school, my feelings about being Native American were ambivalent. I simply hated being *different.* Before kindergarten, my life had been very sheltered. Even though I was aware that I did not look like the other children on our street, I had not given it much thought.

I had not even known I was Native American until I was four years old and a little girl who lived on our block told me. Diane was six years older than I, but we were good friends and played together often. One day when I was at her house, I remarked that my father had been killed in the war. Diane immediately countered, "No, he wasn't! Your parents are *divorced* and your father is an *Indian!*"

I was so shocked I could not even respond. I quickly left for home. While I hurried back to my house, my mind was racing. I thought about the way I looked. I did not look at all like any members of my family. In fact, I did not look like anyone I had ever seen. I wondered if Diane was right—if my father really was an Indian. I assumed wherever he was, he must wear feathers and ride a horse.

For over a year, my favorite comic book had been one about Geronimo. My grandmother never liked that book and told me he had been a bad Indian. She did say that there were also good Indians, but Geronimo was not one of them. I refused to believe her and was very happy years later when I learned that he truly had been a great leader.

As I burst through our back door and into the kitchen, my grandmother was removing a coffee cake from the oven. "Mama!" I yelled. "Diane said that my father wasn't killed in the war. She said he's an Indian and my parents are *divorced!*"

The thought of my parents being divorced concerned me far more than hearing I was Native American. I knew that divorce was scandalous and I feared I would be a social outcast for life.

My grandmother was very upset. "I don't know why Diane would tell you such a thing. Your parents aren't divorced."

I refused to budge until I finally heard her version of the story. My grandmother said that my father did go to war, but he had not been killed. She emphasized that she had been telling the truth when she told me he had not come back. She had not said he was killed, only that he never returned. She believed he was now living in Oklahoma and yes, he might have "a drop of Indian blood somewhere."

She reassured me that my parents were not divorced. She said they were very young when they married and she and my grandfather had the marriage annulled. She said that both of my parents had agreed to this.

Years later, I would find out that when my parents and grandparents were still living in Oklahoma, while my father was at work, my grandparents had picked up my mother from her apartment and fled to California. My father sent the FBI after them, believing they were planning to abort his baby. My grandmother vehemently denied any plans for an abortion, but I was never totally convinced.

I thought annulment sounded better than divorce, so I felt somewhat relieved. I left the kitchen and went straight into the bathroom. I looked into the pink ruffled mirror that sat on the dressing table beneath the window, and I saw a little Indian girl staring back at me. I knew Diane had told the truth.

By the next day, I was happily playing with my friends and life was back to normal. No one ever again questioned who I was—until I started school.

Every day in class I kept my eyes on the clock waiting for the day to end. I longed to be back in the safety of my home or playing with the children on my street. Besides the neighbor children, I had two animal friends that I loved very much. I spent many hours playing with Duke, a German shepherd, and Monkey, a calico cat, who lived down the street from us. I have never accepted the belief that there is a difference in the importance of humans and animals. I believe that Creator made us all, and we each have the right to a happy and safe life here on Earth.

Although my neighbor, Colleen, and my cousin, Jennifer, were in the same grade as I, we were never in the same classroom at school. I guess the teachers were afraid that we would be disruptive if we were in the room together. I kept wishing that we could be in the same class, but that never happened.

At home, I was a complete tomboy. I started riding horses when I was three years old. At four, I could roller-skate so fast that, at night, sparks shot from the metal wheels of my skates as they flew over the concrete sidewalk. I loved a good fistfight with either a boy or a girl, and I could outrun most children my age, and several who were older. I was as much at home in trees as I was on the ground. At the end of our street, there was a huge old walnut tree. I used to climb to one of the highest branches, hang by my knees and then drop, catching myself by my heels, and then continue to dangle there high above the ground. My grandmother would have died if she had known what I was doing.

When a junior college was built behind the houses across the street from us, I used to play there, many times dragging Jennifer with me. I loved to climb up onto the interlocking roofs of the classrooms and run from one roof to the next. Upon hearing my heavy shoes thudding on the roofs, angry students and teachers would pour out onto the walkways. Jennifer, who never could quite make it up onto the roofs, would run, terrified, but I would just laugh and make my getaway onto the next roof. I thought it was great fun. Years later, when Jennifer attended the college, she said she could never enter a classroom without remembering our wild rooftop escapades and laughing about them.

My days at school continued to be miserable. All through elementary school, if I had new pencils, a ruler, or anything another child wanted, I always let him or her have it. The teachers would call my grandmother and tell her that I was giving everything away. I think the teachers thought I was trying to "buy" friendship, but that was not true—I simply didn't want one of my classmates to be sad about anything. I was so desperately unhappy in school that I didn't want any other child to feel as terrible as I did.

In second grade, part of the day was devoted to music. Our teacher decided that each student would sing a few lines alone so that she could determine the range of our voices. I thought I would die when I heard her announce this to the class. I can't sing a note. I'm practically tone deaf, and the thought of doing anything in front of the class was enough to send me into coronary arrest. I was almost hyperventilating when she finally called on me to stand up. I mumbled a few lines and she told me to sing louder. I mumbled a few more lines and she told me to sit down.

After everyone had finished, she began to arrange our singing groups. The girls were on one side of the room and the boys on the other. She made each child stand in a certain place according to voice range. When she came to me she told me to go stand in the boys' group. I thought I must have misunderstood. She couldn't be telling me to stand with all the boys. But that was exactly what she meant. She obviously had the sensitivity and caring typical of most people living in Orange County at that time. I cannot understand how such a person could be turned loose in a room full of children. I stood surrounded by all those boys and wished I were dead.

When I got home and told my grandmother what had happened she went into an absolute rage. She called that teacher and told her exactly what she thought of her. I had never seen my grandmother that mad before. The teacher tried to justify her action by saying that she had put me in the boys' group because I had a low voice. She simply could not understand why I was upset. My grandmother quickly enlightened her, and the next day in music class I was in the girls' group. I'm not sure that the other girls were happy, but I was greatly relieved.

One day I remember falling on the playground. The bell rang to mark the end of recess and all the children started to run toward the school building. Somehow, I tripped and fell flat on my face on the blacktop. The other children ran right over me, as if I were invisible. I felt their heavy oxfords running over my back, and as they stepped on my head, they actually twisted the soles of their shoes to make sure they hurt me as much as possible.

After they finally passed over me, I hurt so much I couldn't even get up. I just lay on the ground, face down, crying and wishing I were home with my grandmother. Suddenly, I heard a concerned voice asking if I was all right and then felt someone gently helping me up. The kind child who helped me was a sixth grade "safety" named Arlene. She took me to the school nurse and then stayed to take me back to my classroom. I thought Arlene was the most beautiful girl I had ever seen. I was sure she was an angel in disguise here on Earth.

Miraculously, in the fourth grade my school days improved. When I started back to school in September, there was a new girl in my class. Her name was Jackie and within two days we became fast friends. Sometimes I would go over to her house after school and other times she would come to mine.

I had never known a household like Jackie's. Her mother was divorced and ran a day care center out of their house. Jackie and I were always interrupted in our play by screaming and yelling preschoolers. Jackie had a little sister in the second grade, but she and Jackie didn't have many toys of their own. Most of the toys were for the children in day care.

After only six months in our school, Jackie moved with her mother and sister to a nearby town. I missed her a lot after she was gone. When I was in junior high school, I heard that when Jackie was in the sixth grade, her mother committed suicide. She had gone into the garage, shut the door, sat on the front seat of the car, and turned on the motor. Those two little girls came home from school and found their mother dead. I felt so sorry for my poor little friend. I don't know what ever happened to Jackie and her sister.

While still in the fourth grade, I managed to make two more friends. First I became friends with Cecilia, a lovely Mexican American girl with beautiful, shiny black hair cut in a dutch-boy bob. She was a very quiet little girl and a straight A student.

Cecilia lived a few blocks away from me and we took turns playing at each other's house after school. Cecilia's house was very similar to mine, always orderly, and her mother carefully supervised our play. Once again, I was happy. I looked forward to going to school each day. I loved Cecilia very much. It was wonderful to have a friend.

Shortly after Cecilia and I became friends, another little girl started to play with us. Her name was Judianne. There were six children in Judianne's family, and her parents were good Christians who really practiced their religion. They had no problem, whatsoever, that Judianne's two best friends were Mexican American and Native American. In fact, in the sixth grade, when some girls started to go steady and wear their boyfriends' rings around their necks, Judianne went steady for a while with Conrad, a quiet, mannerly, and very handsome Mexican American boy. Only Judianne, who had been brought up in a family that would never have tolerated prejudice in any form, would have had the courage to do this at that time in Orange County. Judianne managed to get away with it probably because she was quiet and studious and her family was so highly respected. Anyone else would have been tarred and feathered and run out of town.

Judianne, Cecilia, and I formed a little club, and we moved our club meetings around between our three houses. I could not believe my good fortune—not one friend, but two!

In fifth grade, I became friends with a new girl in our class. I, of course, had no way of looking into the future to see that this little girl would grow up to be a woman who would become a lifelong friend and would actually one day save my life.

Linda and her family, which included her parents, younger sister Maureen, and her mother's Aunt Edna and Uncle Bill, had moved into town from New York. We quickly became best friends and although we are now separated by many miles, we are still as close today.

Linda's house was always warm, happy, and full of laughter. I was a little jealous because Linda shared a bedroom with her sister Maureen. I thought it would be wonderful never to have to be alone. Years later, I learned that Linda had been jealous of me because I was able to have my own room. I guess the old saying is true: The grass is always greener.

Linda and I were both very imaginative young girls. We read science fiction, slept in sleeping bags in my backyard, looked up at the sky with our small binoculars, and felt positive we would be the first women on Mars. We also walked around the school ground reciting *Romeo and Juliet* and I memorized all of *Hiawatha*.

When we were in the sixth grade and Linda had a crush on a boy in our class named Alan, we devised a plan to make him drop his girlfriend and start liking Linda. We made a "candy" heart out of a thick, pink liquid medicine used for upset stomachs as well as several other disgusting ingredients. We wrote a note saying that this was a "love offering" and he should eat it immediately. We signed his girlfriend's name.

Linda spent the night at my house and we sneaked out of my bedroom window, in our shortie nightgowns, and ran the three blocks to Alan's house. We put the "candy" heart on his doorstep, rang the bell, and ran all the way back home.

We were very surprised to see Alan at school the next day. We had hoped that he would be home sick after eating the "candy" heart. Linda had planned to take a get-well card to him, and since he would be mad at his girlfriend for almost poisoning him, he would then start to like Linda.

After school we walked by Alan's house to see if we could figure out what happened to the heart. We quickly realized that in the dark and excitement of the previous night, we had left the heart on his next-door neighbor's front porch. I think Linda gave up on Alan after that.

As I look back on my childhood, I realize how innocent we were. We had never heard of drugs. No one carried a knife larger than a pocketknife, and no one, other than a policeman, carried a gun. Very few mothers worked and divorce was almost unheard of. You could take a walk after dark and not have to worry about being raped or assaulted.

The kids who went steady in the fifth and sixth grades held hands walking home from school and maybe stole an occasional kiss behind someone's garage. I still had no idea where babies came from.

CHAPTER SIX

The Awakening

*No matter how hard I try to forget you, you
always come back to my mind.*

—Nootka love song

*J*unior high school brought major changes to my life.
While some of these changes were positive, others were
extremely painful. By ninth grade, I had convinced myself
that my life was a modern day tragedy. I believed I was the
living embodiment of Juliet, cruely brought back to Earth
to endure a lifetime of suffering.

I know now that my life was following a pathway. All the
things that happened to me were for a reason. I did not
fully understand this until years later when I could pause
and look back over the road I had traveled. It had been
quite a journey.

Remembering my first year in junior high school, I
realize that in seventh grade I was between agony and
ecstacy. The painful early years of grade school were behind me. I now had friends and life was actually fun.

The popular girls in the school were a world away from my little group of friends. These girls were cheerleaders and pompom girls and they were always elected to student body offices. They all had boyfriends, dressed like the girls in high school, used makeup, and wore their hair in the latest styles. They looked far older than other girls in the seventh grade.

I was still a little girl. I knew nothing of fashion—I wore very ordinary cotton dresses. My long, straight, black hair was parted in the middle, pulled back to the nape of my neck, and held in place by a very large, sparkly, ugly barrette. My thick bangs hung to my bushy, black eyebrows. I wore no makeup whatsoever. I gave new meaning to the word "homely."

The only really horrible thing that happened to me in the seventh grade had actually started a year earlier—I had begun to develop breasts. For a little girl who still wanted to remain completely unnoticed, this was very frightening. In order to conceal this problem, I found a very strong band of elastic, and each morning before I dressed, I bound my chest until it was perfectly flat. The tight band was very uncomfortable, but it gave me peace of mind. Somehow, even looking as I did, I managed to attract the attention of a very nice boy in one of my classes. He was blond, short, and a little on the chubby side. I was not overly impressed. He followed me around the school ground every day and finally began to walk me home from school.

We ended up "going steady" for a very brief period of time. My interest in having his ring around my neck was far greater than my interest in him. Every night, we spent about an hour talking on the phone. He once invited me to a carnival and when he arrived at my door, he gave me a huge bottle of cologne that probably cost about a dollar. It was a very sweet gesture, even though it smelled horrible. Once he even kissed me on the cheek.

To my relief, our relationship ended when summer vacation started. I knew there had to be more to romance than this. I had a strong feeling that there was a fabulous young man out there, somewhere, waiting for me. I just had to find him.

I spent the summer after seventh grade fantasizing about finding the boy of my dreams and pasting new pictures into my Tony Curtis scrapbook. I thought that Tony Curtis, who was a big star at that time, was the most handsome man I had ever seen. I read everything I could find about him and his young, beautiful wife, Janet Leigh. In their pictures, they looked very much in love and I made myself a promise to never settle for less.

Before the summer ended, I started a new scrapbook with pictures of James Dean. Now the boy of my dreams had a new dimension. Not only did he have to be exceptionally handsome, but he also had to be a little on the delinquent side—a real rebel, somewhat of a misfit, who didn't care what anyone else thought. It was with these dreams in mind that I returned to school in September.

It was in the eighth grade that my life changed forever. Once childhood is lost, you can never go back. I was thirteen years old.

Back at school my life was no different than it had been the previous year. I still had my same friends and I still looked horrible. After school I hurried home to secretly play with my Toni doll, using little plastic rollers and sugar water to curl her hair.

One day at lunch time, my friend Linda and I were walking around the school ground talking when the conversation somehow turned to the subject of having babies. I stuck by my belief that you certainly didn't need a man to become pregnant. I guess Linda decided that, at my age, I should know better and she quickly filled me in on the facts of life.

I thought I was going to be physically ill. It was the most disgusting thing I had ever heard. For days afterward, I felt sick every time I remembered what Linda had told me. I was sure she was wrong. I knew if what she said was true, the world's population would have died out long ago.

Between classes at school, safetys were posted at each corner of the hallway. The safetys were chosen from the honor students, and their job was to prevent anyone from running or shoving in the hallways. As I started to pass Gretchen, a safety who was in the ninth grade, I stopped dead in my tracks. Walking toward us was the most gorgeous boy I had ever seen. His hair was black and cut in a style very similar to the way Tony Curtis wore his. He had hazel eyes, long eyelashes, and an absolutely perfect face. He wore jeans and walked with a confident swagger.

"Hi, kiddo," he said to Gretchen, as he smiled and winked at her. Gretchen returned his smile. "Hi, Allen."

I could hardly breathe as I watched him walk away down the hall. When he was finally out of sight, I turned back to Gretchen. "Gretchen, who was that?" I asked in a weak voice.

Gretchen looked at me as if I had suddenly asked what country we were in. "Don't you know who Allen is?" she asked incredulously. "He's the most popular boy in school. Probably the whole town."

"Oh," was all I could say. I walked to my class in a daze. From that moment on, my life would never be the same.

When I got home from school, I went directly to my room and closed the door. I lay on the bed and began to plot. If Allen was to ever notice me, I would have to make some definite changes.

The next day at school I spent the entire day studying the dress and demeanor of the girls in the popular crowd. After school, I got some money from GoGo, who was a teacher at the school, and went shopping downtown. When I arrived at school the next morning, in no way did

I resemble the girl of the previous day. I had thrown away my breast-binding elastic. My little cotton dresses had been traded in for a tight skirt and sweater. I threw away the ugly barrette, curled the ends of my long hair, and let it fall freely to my waist. My eyebrows, which could previously have been mistaken for two large black caterpillars, had been carefully, painfully plucked. I was wearing makeup. I have seen many "make-overs" on television. Never have I seen such a drastic change as I had managed to accomplish.

Many of the boys at school noticed me that day. Some of them actually asked if I was new at school. For the first time in my life, I began to feel confident and when I looked in the mirror, I no longer saw an ugly face staring back at me. The only boy who didn't seem to notice me at all was Allen.

Finally, after much effort, plotting, and scheming on my part, Allen did notice me and we fell madly, deeply in love. I was almost fourteen; Allen was fifteen. This was not "puppy love." This was the kind of love that's written about in romance novels or that you see in the movies, but never seems to happen in real life. But it did happen. I loved Allen with every fiber of my being. Then tragedy struck. Allen's mother was diagnosed with cancer and she quickly became very ill. Almost every minute that he was not in school he spent taking care of his mother. He told me that he had to get up many times during the night to take water to her or comfort her. Allen and his father did not have a good relationship.

My grandparents did not like Allen at all. He was very polite, had a brilliant mind, made good grades, was a devoted son to his mother, and loved me with all his heart. My grandparents said he was too old for me. He was a grade ahead of me and seventeen months older.

What really upset my grandparents was Allen's maturity. He was confident, determined, and far older than his fifteen years. My grandparents tried to keep me away from him, but there was nothing on Earth, short of putting us in prison, that could have kept us apart.

Things quickly got worse. Allen's mother died and his father decided to move to a town more than an hour's drive away. I felt as if my life had ended. Allen was too young to get a driver's license, but that didn't stop him from driving his father's car and seeing me as often as possible.

It wasn't long into Allen's junior year that the situation with his father became untenable. Unable to get along with his father, he moved out, got his own apartment, and worked his way through both high school and college. He received letters in football, excelled as an amateur boxer, and played his violin at night in a gypsy cafe where every woman in the room was dying to go home with him. My grandparents tried and tried to separate us, but distance finally accomplished what my grandparents could not. We saw less and less of each other, but our love remained strong.

Since I was Allen's girlfriend, I now ran around with the popular crowd. We did a lot of really crazy things and had a wonderful time. I had quite a few "temporary" boyfriends, but Allen still had his hand firmly on my heart.

In the ninth grade, I got a terrible crush on one of our coaches who looked very much like Yul Brynner. Fortunately, he was either too cowardly or had too much sense to do anything about it. I was fourteen. He was thirty-two.

Since his idol was Sophia Loren, I decided to change my image. At that time, all of the girls at school, when not wearing tight skirts, wore full ones ballooned out by stiffly starched petticoats. The petticoats crackled while we walked, and when not being worn, were able to easily stand alone.

I had just seen Sophia Loren in a movie and immediately decided I wanted to look just like she did. I threw out my petticoats and let my full cotton skirts hang in natural folds. I pulled my seventeen-inch waist in even tighter with a wide leather belt. My long black hair hung to my waist. I thinned out my bangs and let them hang in separate strands, the way Sophia's bangs had looked in the movie. I learned to use black eyeliner and wore pale, natural lipstick. I wore the barest sandals I could find.

I stopped smiling and tried to look sultry. Instead of demurely crossing my ankles while sitting, I now sat with my legs apart, my skirt hanging down between my knees. I was sure that if I were only six inches taller, I would be mistaken for Sophia Loren.

The coach definitely noticed. He flirted with me a lot and stared at me continuously, but that was as far as it went. By coincidence, when I went on to high school, he became the high school football coach.

Through all of the crazy, fun-filled days of my last year in junior high school, Allen was always on my mind. He came to see me several times, but distance was still our greatest enemy.

Looking back from the vantage point of time, I believe that if Allen had not moved away, we would have eventually married and I would have left the path that I was born to follow. Sometimes, even the most painful things in our lives happen for a reason. Many times, without knowing it, in our darkest hours, we are being guided and led forward.

CHAPTER SEVEN

The Challenge

I have found my love. Oh, I think it is so!

—Chippewa love song

The first year of high school went rather slowly. We still did crazy things, like going over to a boy's house at night to write on his car with soap or sneak our parents' car out of the garage after they were asleep to cruise Main Street. Cruising Main Street was an absolute necessity in our lives. Only a certain part of the street was "cool" to cruise. It began at a gas station that was owned by a man with three handsome sons, two of whom were in high school and one a couple of years older, and ended at a drive-through hamburger stand that we called the "in and out."

We felt very grown-up. We went to a lot of parties, read best-selling novels that were considered to be a little "racy," studied top fashion magazines, and wrote poetry. My girlfriend, Charlotte, and I drank her father's peppermint schnapps, putting it in grape juice, and then filling the schnapps bottle with water.

I had several different boyfriends, but none could begin to compete with Allen until my junior year of high school. We had four or five new young teachers that year. Since my girlfriends and I were so full of ourselves and believed our maturity to be far beyond our teenage years, we naturally developed crushes on the teachers.

Some of my girlfriends kept telling me that one of the new coaches, Pete, always stared at me. I didn't even know who he was, but I soon found out. When a friend pointed him out to me I saw that he was tall, well-built, and handsome, with beautiful, big, green eyes. With all the false confidence you can have only when you are fifteen, I decided that since this man was interested in me I'd show him a thing or two. The next time I caught him looking at me, I did my best to appear worldly and sexy; I openly stared back at him. His eyes challenged me to return his interest, and looking back at him, I accepted that challenge.

Although Pete knew how old I was, I did look a year or two older than my fifteen years. I later learned that he had a strong attraction to large-breasted women. This may have been one of the reasons that he first noticed me. Although my waist had grown by three inches in the past two years, my figure was still holding firm at 39-20-34. I thanked God for a small waist and large breasts that I used to so carefully bind.

Before Christmas of my junior year, I was sure he was finally going to ask to see me outside of school, but, before that happened, fate intervened. I received a call from Pete's cousin, Phil, who was a year behind me in school and happened to be one of my best friends. He explained that Pete had received a severe injury to his eyes in a water skiing accident and was in the hospital.

I was devastated. I wanted desperately to see him, but I knew I had to be very careful. Even though our relationship had never gone past flirting, if school authorities even guessed what was going on, I would be out of school and he would be out of a job.

In Santa Ana, in the '50s, a teacher dating a student might well have ended with a lynching. The dean of girls at our high school was so strict that we were forbidden to wear patent leather shoes for fear they would act as a mirror for boys to look up our dresses. We were not allowed to wear open-toed sandals because they were considered too suggestive. Yet, after Pete and I dared to start seeing each other, four or five other young teachers also started dating students. One even went to jail for statutory rape after his young girlfriend became pregnant.

After much thought, I devised a plot that I was sure would get me safely into the hospital to see Pete. I called Phil and asked him to take me into the hospital posing as his girlfriend. He firmly refused, worried that his family would find out and we would both get into a lot of trouble. Finally, after much pleading, he agreed to go along with my wild scheme.

When we arrived at the hospital, I felt like a spy involved in great intrigue. When we encountered family members in the hallway, Phil had his arm around my shoulders and introduced me as his girlfriend. I had butterflies in my stomach and my heart was pounding as we entered the hospital room.

I could only stare at this man lying on the bed with its perfectly folded white sheets. The room was dimly lit and totally silent. Phil and I walked across the room until we stood next to the bed.

"Hi, it's Phil," Phil said in a soft voice, "and I have someone with me." I couldn't take my eyes from Pete's face lying on the pillow. His eyes were bandaged and he had several days' growth of beard. He looked like an injured soldier out of a wartime movie. He was so very different from the boys at school. My heart jumped as I heard his husky voice ask, "Who's with you?"

In a soft, low voice that surprisingly sounded very sexy, I answered, "Guess?"

He smiled slightly as he said my name. At that moment, I stopped playing and started really caring.

The next day I was somewhat of a heroine among my few friends who knew about my hospital adventure. We thought it was extremely romantic and daring. I had no way of knowing that this was an important step on the pathway that had been chosen for my life.

In March of my junior year, my romance with the football coach finally moved out of the high school corridors. He asked me to meet him at the beach on Saturday. He chose a spot by the Newport pier, where no one we knew ever went. I agreed to go and immediately began to worry if it would be acceptable to call him by his first name.

I was now sixteen and fortunately had a driver's license. GoGo had bought an old Ford for me to drive to and from school. As I made the half-hour drive to the beach, I felt grown-up, seductive, and glamorous. I was also a nervous wreck.

I spread my new beach towel on the sand, sat down, and waited for Pete to arrive. I was glad he had chosen this remote location. I was sure that, at his age, he would be white and flabby, and wear old man's swim trunks. Even though I desperately wanted to see him, it would be a little embarrassing to be seen publicly with someone who looked like that.

It was past the time that we had agreed to meet, and I began to worry that maybe he had changed his mind. I looked around the beach and then up at the pier. I saw him standing, leaning against the railing, looking down at me, and smiling. I smiled back.

I was both shocked and relieved by his appearance. He was deeply tanned and muscular, and wearing well-fitted, turquoise swim trunks. He looked like a young god. It was hard to believe that he could look so fantastic. He was twenty-three years old.

The rest of high school was wonderful. I couldn't wait to get to school every day. I had my routes between classes organized so that I would pass Pete in the halls as often as possible, which allowed us to secretly pass notes to each other. My study hall teacher, who was a friend of Pete's and knew we were seeing each other, used to send me on imaginary errands so that I would be able to slip into the teacher's study to see Pete during his free period.

My English class was on the second floor in a room with windows looking toward the football field. Every day, at the same time, the coaches walked back from the gym to the main building. Each day, at that exact time, I walked past the windows to the pencil sharpener. It became a ritual—Pete would stop on the walkway and look up, and I would pause at the window and look down. We would smile at each other and I would feel such happiness.

When I learned that the Future Faculty Club had a yearly banquet where students were allowed to bring a teacher as a guest, I quickly joined the club. One of my girlfriends who was interested in another young coach joined the club with me. We were obviously not Future Faculty Club material. We didn't know another person in the club. Everyone looked at us very suspiciously, wondering whatever possessed us to join.

The night of the banquet was hysterical. Pete and the other coach, Bob, were picking us up at my house. We spent hours getting ready. I think my grandparents were a little suspicious, but since the event was sanctioned by the school, they really couldn't say anything.

When we walked into the banquet room, every eye was on us. We were the only students that had brought teachers of the opposite sex. My girlfriend and I looked very grown-up and sophisticated and looked more like the coaches' dates than their students.

We made the mistake of sitting by two young, female physical education teachers. These two unattractive women kept trying to talk to Pete and Bob who simply ignored them and continued to talk and laugh with us. To say that the whole room was abuzz with gossip was an understatement.

Before we went back to my house later that night, the four of us stopped at a coffee shop for milk shakes. If we had not previously been at a totally legitimate school function, we would never have dared to be seen in public.

While we were laughing, talking, and enjoying our milk shakes, we looked up to see one of the school's singing groups enter the restaurant. They must have been performing somewhere that evening because the teacher who was in charge of the group was with them. We tried to ignore them, but I was a little nervous because I knew that one of the girls in the group was a vicious gossip. Her name was Alex and she was a popular senior at school. She had bleached white hair, which she wore in a ponytail, and never had one hair out of place. She was a cute girl, but in an attempt to cover a bad complexion, she wore so much makeup it looked as though she'd have to scrape it off with a knife.

Alex never took her eyes off of us until we left to go home. No one knew about the Future Faculty Club banquet, so naturally she assumed we were simply out on a date. Of course, in truth, she was right.

The next morning, Alex was busy spreading gossip all over the school. She said that she had seen the four of us in a bar the night before and that I was passed out on the barroom floor. I guess no one bothered to ask what she was doing in a bar.

I was furious. I confronted her on the school steps and told her about the club banquet. She finally backed down and admitted that she had really seen us in a coffee shop. Of course the whole school had already heard the rumor. Pete was so mad that he immediately renamed her "poison ivy" and, from that time on, never referred to her by any other name.

In October of my senior year, Pete and I decided to have a child. Although it was almost unheard of at the time, we intended to have our child without the sanctity of marriage. All that mattered was that we loved each other and we wanted a baby.

From the moment we made that decision, it became the most important thing in my life. I prayed that I would have a son, as Pete wished. I tried to eat well and take good care of myself so that my body would be strong enough to carry our unborn child.

I knew that I was very young to be a mother, but I was determined to do everything right. I bought books on child rearing, which I studied voraciously. Every one of the books emphasized the importance of a child growing up within the security of a stable family structure. The more I read, the more I worried. I began to wonder if I was making a mistake by having a child without Pete and I being married.

I considered discussing this with Pete, but decided against it. I was painfully aware that I was still only sixteen, and I was afraid he would think that I was acting immaturely.

With the thought of parenthood constantly on my mind, I began to wonder about my own father. The only thing I had ever known about him was that he was Indian and probably lived in Oklahoma. This was not much to go on, but I made up my mind to find him.

Over much protest, I enlisted the aid of my grandparents, and we began making a long series of telephone calls to Oklahoma. After about four weeks and a very expensive telephone bill, we finally succeeded in finding someone who knew where he was living. My grandmother left her name, along with our phone number, and a message for him to return her call.

When my father did call, it was a very emotional conversation. We both cried and he asked me to come to Oklahoma to visit so that we could finally get to know each other. He told me that he was remarried and that his wife and their two sons were also looking forward to meeting me. I was elated. I believed he would be the perfect, loving father. My expectations were not met.

I spent my seventeenth birthday in Oklahoma City with my father, his wife, and their two sons. Mike was about four years younger than I, and like his mother, was very sweet and gentle. Steve was a couple of years younger than his brother, and not only looked very much like me but had a similar personality. I immediately loved my brothers and knew that neither time nor distance would ever change that love.

During this first visit with my father, he appeared to be everything I had expected—a very proud and loving father. He had taken a week's vacation, driven me everywhere, and introduced me to friends and relatives, who all commented on how much we looked alike.

When I looked at my father it was almost as if I were looking into a mirror. I saw his high school yearbook and his pictures could easily have been photos of me with a man's haircut. I wondered if that was the reason my mother had left me with my grandparents. She probably couldn't look at me without seeing my father.

During the next six years, I saw my father and his family three or four more times. In between those visits, we stayed in touch by phone or letter. When I decided to move to Los Angeles, he asked me to come back to Oklahoma and attend college. I thanked him, but explained that I had already made definite plans to move to Los Angeles.

That was the last I ever heard from him. I learned that the one thing no one could do was disagree with my father. My refusal to move to Oklahoma ended our relationship. After my automobile accident in 1969, a friend of mine called my father and told him that his daughter was dying. His *only* response was, "Is she still living in Los Angeles?"

My father was not raised with traditional Native American values and I believe he would have been happier if he had been born Caucasian. During the time he was growing up it was especially difficult for a Native American in a predominantly white society. That does not excuse his treatment of me or, as I later learned, the extremely harsh discipline of my brothers.

What I regret most about my separation from my father is that it made it impossible to see my brothers while they were growing up. I continued to love and miss them, and when they were grown, Steve and I managed to occasionally phone each other. Through these phone calls I was able to keep up-to-date with my brothers' lives, while keeping them abreast of my own. After tragically losing my brother Mike to cancer, Steve and I have renewed our vows to always stay in touch.

In the spring, as the time we had chosen for conception drew closer, both Pete and I anxiously looked forward to having a baby. Whenever I passed him on the school ground, I had to laugh because he was always eating raisins—he had told me that he heard somewhere that raisins make a man fertile.

We chose a night that we believed would be easiest for me to conceive. I met him at the beach, and surrounded by fresh salt air and the sound of the pounding surf, our son was conceived. During my pregnancy, Pete was wonderful. He told me over and over that he thought I looked beautiful and took me into the beach bars to show me off to his friends.

I was determined to have natural childbirth, although my doctor said my bones were so narrow that I would probably have to have a Cesarean section. At that time, it was standard procedure for a doctor to give a woman everything possible during childbirth to ease the pain. However, I had read a book about natural childbirth, and believing it would be best for the baby, no one could change my mind.

I experienced all the pain of natural childbirth, but none of the joy. I had 9½ hours of very hard labor. I refused all medication. I made the nurse tie a bedsheet to the end of the bed. I held on to the sheet, braced my feet against the bed's footboard, and bore down. I knew I was doing everything right. The nurse told me that the baby's head had crowned, and at that point, the pain never stopped. There was no more pausing between contractions. Only women who have had children without any anesthetic understand the pain at the moment of birth. Since I obviously was not built for childbirth, my pain was even greater.

The doctor allowed me to lie there, with the crown of my baby's head actually pushed through, for 18½ more hours. The pain was so great that I was finally going in and out of consciousness. My greatest fear was that my baby might die. I was also afraid that the hours of extreme pressure on his little head might cause brain damage. Even before my child was born, his welfare came before all other things in my life.

Even though I was in critical condition, the doctor announced that he did not work between 10:00 P.M. and 6:00 A.M. and left. When he arrived back at the hospital at 6:00 A.M., I remember the nurses actually running, with me on a gurney, down the hall toward the operating room. I was dying.

Things were then moving so fast that, at the same time the anesthesiologist was giving me a spinal block, I felt the doctor cutting into my stomach. Then I felt nothing—the pain was gone. I remember telling the anesthesiologist that I thought he was the most wonderful man on Earth.

I heard a baby crying and then the doctor held him above my head. I looked up at a perfect baby boy who, of course, would be named "Pete," after his father. My prayers were answered; I had a son. It was the greatest moment of my life.

I slept for more than twenty-four hours. When I awakened, I was so weak that the nurse had to prop me up with pillows and help me hold my baby. I wanted to breastfeed, but I had no milk. When I laid on my back I did not even have the strength to turn onto my side.

The next day I began to run a fever so high that I slipped in and out of consciousness. Although it was midday and not visiting hours, my grandparents suddenly appeared, and other family members were standing in the doorway of my hospital room. A nurse brought my baby into the room, and I realized she believed she was showing him to me for the last time. Once again, I was dying.

The family left when an orderly came in to move me into another room. He wheeled me into a small room that was far from the rest of the patients. I knew I had been taken to this room to die.

During the rest of the day and night, the nurses kept going in and out of my room giving me shots. One gave me a blood transfusion. Nothing could bring the fever down.

The night nurse was a very kind person. She sat beside my bed changing cold compresses on my forehead. When she took a cold wet towel and tried to smooth my hair back from my face, my hair began to fall out by the handfuls. (I guess this was a result of the high fever.) The nurse began crying. I heard her talking to someone else, mentioning temperatures of 105 and 106 degrees. I again lost consciousness.

The next day I was surprised I was still alive. I was too weak to move and I kept thinking of my son and his father. I didn't want to leave them. I had to live, but I was too weak to even try.

Pete, who never did have much patience, finally issued an order that probably saved my life. With his firm, authoritarian voice, he ordered me to get well. He told me that I was not going to die. He wanted me to get well and out of that bed. He said that no one else was going to raise his son. I heard a lot of love in that order and I began to fight.

My fever broke and I was moved back into a room with other patients. Every time a nurse came into the room, I asked to have my baby brought to me. I was still too weak to hold him without help.

Two days later, I was able to hold on to the bed rails and turn myself from my back to my side—to make that small turn took one-half hour. For me, it was a great feat. I knew I was getting better.

I was truly happy and Pete was ecstatic that the baby was a boy. After I recovered, life seemed free from any cares. I believed the future would be perfect. I had just turned eighteen and Pete was twenty-five.

About a year later, Pete and I went our separate ways without ever completely separating. For many years, from time to time, we would find our way back into each other's arms.

CHAPTER EIGHT

A Teenager's Dream

*My heart laughs with joy because I am in
your presence.*

—a Chitmachas chief, early 1700s

I was now alone with a year-old baby and no job or work experience. I was barely nineteen. I had enough money saved to get a two-bedroom apartment and immediately began looking for work.

After many rejections, I found a job in a plant just outside of town. All I remember about that job, which involved routine paperwork, was that it was terribly boring and I hated it. We had to wear identification badges and punch a time clock. I felt like Rosie the Riveter.

Even though I was fortunate to find a good babysitter with whom I could leave Pete every morning, I still cried all the way to work. It was so painful to have to be away from my baby that I could hardly stand it. I called the babysitter on my morning and afternoon breaks and during the forty-five minutes I had for lunch.

One day when I made my morning break call, the babysitter said Pete had just taken his first steps. I was heartbroken. I was stuck working in a plant, missing out on all the wonderful things a mother should experience with her child.

Pete was a happy baby who never cried or fussed. The babysitter commented many times that she had never known such a good baby. I was very lucky.

Every morning as I dressed for work, I would look at myself in the mirror and realize that I was the only thing between Pete and hunger. The thought terrified me.

It was not long before I was able to change jobs. I was hired as the manager of the costume jewelry section at a major department store. I was glad to be in pleasant surroundings and out of that horrible plant. The only positive thing that came out of my plant experience was that while working there I had made a good friend. Bobbie was married and after four daughters she and her husband gave up trying to have a son. Her daughters later became babysitters for Pete and many times took him on their family outings. A few years later, Pete was the ring bearer in Bobbie's oldest daughter's wedding.

My job at the department store created a major problem because it required me to work some evenings. The babysitter I was using could only watch Pete during the day. The problem was solved when a girlfriend agreed to move in and care for Pete. I paid for everything, including her food, and gave her a small weekly salary. She and I got along fine and Pete was well taken care of. The only problem I had was money. There now was another mouth to feed.

I quickly devised a plan that worked quite well. I went through my list of eligible male friends and let them know I was available for lunch. I set up a schedule where I had lunch with a different man each day of the week. These became regular weekly lunch dates. It only used up seven men on my list. I made another list for dinner dates.

At both lunch and dinner, I ordered huge meals, ate very little, and took a doggy bag home for my son and babysitter. Fortunately, at that time, I was being asked out quite often. My dates were usually men whom I considered strictly friends. Whenever I found myself short on money, I would refuse a date, explaining that I would love to go out, but I simply couldn't afford to pay a babysitter. Of course, the man always offered to pay. At the end of the evening, before my date would walk me up to my apartment, I would sweetly remind him that I needed twenty dollars for the babysitter (an exorbitant amount at that time).

Claiming that I would be embarrassed if the sitter knew my date was paying her fees, I always insisted that he give me the money before we reached my door. The men always paid without complaint. When we reached the door, it was immediately opened by my smiling babysitter who dutifully refused to leave until my date walked back to his car.

The few times that one of the men didn't seem too anxious to leave, I would ask him if he would like to come in for a little while. Then while he and I sat on one end of the couch, my babysitter would sit on the other end watching television.

One evening, my date stared at the sitter, who was intently watching television, wearing a big robe, with her red hair in rollers and her arms folded across her chest. "What is she, your bodyguard?" he asked in an aggravated voice.

The sitter turned, smiled at him, and went back to watching the television. The man quickly left.

As frightening as the responsibilities of those days were, they were actually fun. I remember one time I had five dates in one day—two were for fun, three were for food.

Pete's father and I still had strong feelings for each other and continued to get together at least a few times every month. I always enjoyed being with him and wanted to keep him in our son's life as much as possible. He had recently decided to open a beer bar, so he quit coaching to take a more lucrative job as a salesman and driver for a food company. I envied his ability to pursue the work of his choice. At the time, I could see no way out of my low-paying job at the department store.

When I came home from work one evening, my sitter asked if we could possibly get another babysitter for Saturday night. She said that a guy she had been dating was back in town and she would like me to drive her up to Hollywood to see him. When I said I'd try, she casually added that he lived with Elvis Presley.

I stared at her in disbelief. I thought she was joking. She convinced me that she was telling the truth. The man she was seeing was part of Elvis' "Memphis mafia." He and Elvis had been close friends since they were very young.

I had been a big Elvis fan since I was thirteen years old. In junior high school, I even started an Elvis Presley fan club. Once a week on our club day, all of the girls wore matching skirts and sweaters to school. It turned out we were so interested in our own boyfriends that the club didn't last very long. But I remained a faithful fan of "the king." I had vowed I would meet him before I turned twenty.

At this moment my life took on new meaning. I could think of nothing but Saturday night. I couldn't sleep all week and I shook constantly. I was finally going to meet Elvis Presley.

About six o'clock Saturday evening, we took off in my old Nash Rambler for Hollywood. My car, which I had bought from a girlfriend for $35, was in such bad condition that we had to stop several times for water before finally pulling off the freeway into Hollywood. We headed up Sunset Boulevard toward Bel Air.

When we drove through the gates of Bel Air, my heart was pounding wildly. We drove up Bellagio Drive and turned through two huge iron gates onto a dark driveway. We parked in front of a beautiful old mansion. Some outside lights came on as we made our way to the front door.

The door opened and we were greeted warmly by several men as we walked into the large formal foyer. It looked more like a hotel than a house.

I was introduced to the men, most of whom had southern accents. They were very friendly and smiled and shook hands. I was so nervous that I knew I would never remember a name or a face. This was the early '60s, I was a teenager, and I was in Elvis Presley's house. I was in an absolute daze.

We walked down a dark stairway into a very large room. Several young men and women were sitting on chairs and couches that lined the walls. At one end of the room was a screen so large that it could have been in a movie theater. There was also a pool table.

As I started to walk to a chair to sit down, I was accosted by Scatter, Elvis' chimpanzee. Scatter looked absolutely darling; he was wearing little shorts and a shirt. In the next second, however, that darling little creature grabbed me around the knees, knocked me to the floor, and tried to pull up my skirt. This was obviously something Scatter had been trained to do and everyone was having a great time laughing at my predicament.

Scatter's strength was incredible, and while I wasn't frightened, I was concerned about what he planned to do once he pulled up my skirt. I was relieved when some of the guys led him away. I tried to pull myself back together as best I could while I quickly found a chair and sat down.

The room was filled with laughter and easy conversation. Several of the guys talked to me and I responded, but I can't remember a word I said. I could only think of one thing: I wanted to see Elvis.

During a moment when no one was talking to me, I suddenly felt a presence in the room. It was as if something very exciting was going on, yet nothing was happening. I turned and looked at the dark stairwell that led up to the main floor of the house. Standing near the bottom of the stairs, framed in dim light, was Elvis Presley and he was looking directly at me.

My heart stopped and then quickly started again, beating a mile a minute. He was much more handsome than in his movies or any of his pictures. To this day, I can't remember what he was wearing. I can only remember that fabulous face.

Elvis was smiling as he walked toward me. I prayed I would not faint. The next thing I knew, Elvis was sitting on my lap with his arm around my shoulders. He started making jokes about how we went to high school together in Memphis. I immediately developed a southern accent and played along with the joke. I had no idea what I was even saying. All I could think about was that Elvis Presley was sitting on my lap. I was still afraid I might faint, and my heart was pounding so hard I was sure everyone in the room could hear it.

Before Elvis got up to play pool with the rest of the guys, he leaned over and kissed me. I thought that if I died at that moment my life would have been complete.

During the rest of the evening, Elvis and I talked more and more. My sitter had warned me that Elvis didn't date girls with children so I was careful not to mention that I had a child. In fact, I hardly said anything of significance, afraid I might say something that would not meet with his approval. Before I left, one of the guys asked for my phone number, explaining that Elvis would like to have it. At that moment, I felt that I was the luckiest girl in the entire world.

In the next couple of months, my sitter and I made several trips to Bel Air while she continued to see Elvis' friend. I did not trust that man and thought he was a real jerk. My suspicions proved to be true when years later he wrote a very unkind book about Elvis. So much for true friendship and loyalty. Elvis would never have done such a thing to one of his friends.

Each visit with Elvis seemed to be more wonderful than the last. This continued until my sitter had to move back home to help take care of her little brother. I didn't have the courage to go to Elvis' uninvited. I felt my life was over.

Soon after that, one of Elvis' friends called and said that Elvis would like me to come up for the evening. Fortune had once again smiled upon me. I saw Elvis quite a few times over the next year or so. He was absolutely gorgeous, had a perfect build, and was a completely kind and thoughtful person.

It was a wonderful and memorable time in my life. I'm glad I had sense enough not to believe I was in love with him, which could only have ended in pain. But I definitely had a strong case of infatuation. After all, I was only nineteen years old and he was Elvis Presley.

CHAPTER NINE

Home at Last

There comes a time in human events when abandonment of racial responsibilities becomes very oppressive, unbearable, intolerable, and there seems to be no hope . . . then man must exert himself, speak and act

—Wassaja, M.D., Mohave Apache, 1915

I worked at the department store only a few months before I was fired. Although I had no trouble selling, I simply could not arrange the display cases. I have no artistic talent whatsoever, and my cases were a disaster. A woman from the hat department helped me for a while until she was fired for being drunk at work. A week later, I was terminated.

My life seemed to be going from bad to worse. For the first time in my life, I now understood real hunger. I made sure that Pete always ate very well, but there were days when I had very little food, and some days none at all. I had to wear decent clothes in order to work, but every day I had to put cardboard over the holes in my six dollar shoes.

Then two things happened that showed me how unimportant material problems really are. Within less than a two-year period, I lost both Mama Big and GoGo. My grief was overwhelming. They had been such an important part of my life that the emptiness was enormous.

I believed that Creator had given me my son so that I would have something to live for. No matter how great my grief, I had a child to take care of and I knew I had to be strong for him. Trying to work when you are grieving is very hard, but I had no choice.

Before Pete was even two years old, he seemed to understand that he and I were facing life alone. While only a toddler, he began to help me in any way that he could. We had a front-loading combination washer/dryer. Pete would stand in front of it, take his diapers from their pail, and put them into the machine. He was not much taller than the diaper pail. Life was not easy for either of us.

After the department store, my next job was as a receptionist/secretary at an advertising agency. The people I worked for were nice, friendly, and patient, but I was terribly overworked. I was secretary to a vice president, two account executives, one part-time account executive, an art director, and the vice president's sister, Jeanne. I can't remember what title Jeanne had. She wrote copy for various accounts and also rewrote much of the copy for the male account executives. She should have been an account executive and received a higher salary, but this was the early '60s and the plight of women in the work force was even worse than it is today.

All in all, it was not a bad job. I did a little modeling for the art director who looked more like a football player than an artist. Although I have absolutely no artistic talent, I do appreciate art. I enjoyed modeling with the smell of oil paint in the room. I imagined I was back in Montmartre at the turn of the century. It was a nice fantasy.

Looking back at my time spent at the ad agency, only three things really stand out in my mind. The first one is a framed ad that hung in my boss' office. It was a full color, center spread ad from a major magazine—a very, very expensive piece of advertising for wristwatches. It showed 100 men dressed in Santa Claus suits. They stood looking straight ahead, each man holding up a clenched fist with the back of the hand facing outward. On each wrist was a watch.

When my boss saw the ad, he said he knew that 100 men could not stand with a clenched fist without one of them making an obscene gesture. He was right. He made a red circle around the fist with the upraised middle finger. At the bottom of the ad he wrote "proofread, proofread, and proofread again!!!"

For the money spent on that one advertisement you could have paid cash for one or two houses at that time. As a result of seeing that ad on my boss' wall every day, I tried to be as meticulous as possible with the work I did at the office.

The second thing I clearly remember is something that never should have happened. I entered into a minor and very unwise office romance with one of the young account executives. Ted was married, with several children, and his wife was once again pregnant. I felt guilty about seeing a married man, but it did make work at the office more interesting. When he complained that he couldn't understand how his wife kept getting pregnant, I knew our relationship would never become intimate.

Our dating ended by mutual consent after one catastrophic night at the opera. Ted had four opera tickets, and he invited me to go with him and another married man, George. George was director of public relations for one of our major accounts. Ted asked if I knew anyone who would like to use the extra ticket. He assured me that this was not to be a date for George; he simply hated to waste a ticket.

It so happened that a girlfriend of mine, Deanna, was in town for a short visit, so I invited her to join us for dinner and the opera. Deanna accepted, and after I got off work we met the men at a restaurant, which was the first mistake. The restaurant Ted chose for our dinner was one that was frequented by all of the advertising people in town.

The four of us were seated in a booth and the waiter had just put our food on the table when George said in a very tense voice, "Don't say anything. Here comes my wife."

Deanna and I thought he was joking. We looked up to see a woman who strongly resembled a low-priced hooker stomping across the room. We still didn't think of trying to leave the table. After all, Deanna was not with George. His wife was welcome to join us.

The second mistake of the evening had taken place when Deanna ordered lobster that was cut up in a thick red sauce. As George's wife descended upon us, we all stopped eating. This crazy woman stopped in front of our table and without saying a word, picked up the heavy restaurant platter with the lobster on it and broke it over Deanna's head. A cup of hot coffee flew into my lap and spilled all over the new dress I was wearing.

Ted jumped up and pulled me out of the booth. Deanna was still sitting in shock with pieces of lobster in her hair and red sauce dripping down onto her shoulders. George scrambled to his feet and grabbed his wife by her shoulders, trying to move her away from the table. Everyone in the restaurant was looking at us. The maitre d' came running across the room and quickly ushered us out through the kitchen and into the parking lot.

As we walked to Ted's car, we heard a woman's loud, angry voice. We saw George, his wife, and the president of George's company standing near the entrance to the restaurant. George's wife was screaming and waving her arms and telling her husband's boss that a horrible account executive from our ad agency had tried to set her husband up with some young girl. Somehow, I had the feeling that this was not the first time that George's wife had found him with another woman.

We went on to the opera, stopping first in a restroom where I was able to get the coffee out of my dress. Deanna had to almost completely wash her hair, and the red sauce had made permanent stains on her blue and white dress.

At the opera we tried to ignore the obvious stares as we walked in. The skirt of my dress was very wet and Deanna's hair was practically dripping. We attempted to act as if nothing were wrong. Looking back on the whole incident, it really was quite funny. However, that night I could find no humor in the situation at all.

I dreaded going into the office the next morning. I was afraid that George's wife had probably called my boss to complain about the incident. I hoped I could avoid even seeing my boss until at least the afternoon; however, only a couple of minutes after I sat down at my desk, the intercom buzzed and my boss asked me to come in and pick up some papers. I felt sick. I walked into his office and tried to act "normal." He greeted me, smiling, and handed me a stack of papers. I turned to walk away, relieved that he obviously knew nothing about the night before.

Just before I reached the doorway, he stopped me. "Oh, by the way, I heard you had a nice time at the opera last night."

I thought I would die. I turned and looked at him. He was smiling broadly and his eyes were twinkling. I gave him a rather sick smile and walked quickly back to my desk. I later learned from Ted that, indeed, George's wife had called my boss and claimed that his employees were plotting to ruin her marriage.

Later that day, I had to type a business letter from Ted to George. I typed the letter and Ted signed it. When the postman delivered our mail, he took the letter to George, along with the rest of our outgoing mail.

It is standard procedure, in most offices, for a secretary to open all of her boss' mail, mark it with the date received, and put it on his desk. So I'm sure George's secretary saw the letter I had typed. I'm also sure that his secretary and everyone else working at George's company knew about the episode in the restaurant.

The next day, as I was filing my carbon copy of the letter I sent to George, I noticed a horrible error. I had meant to type his title—Director of Public Relations—on the letter. To my horror, I noticed that I had left the letter "l" out of the word "public."

My third memorable experience at the ad agency was devastating. I was sitting at my desk one morning when Madeline, the secretary from the insurance office next door, ran through our front door crying. President Kennedy had been assassinated. It was a terrible day. Most of the offices in our complex closed immediately, but ours, being a Republican stronghold, stayed open.

The death of President Kennedy made me realize how vulnerable we all are. Even the president of the United States, with Secret Service men to protect him, could be taken at a young age. I thought about my life and the work I was doing. I strongly believed I was meant to be something other than a secretary. I decided to find another line of work and also, when possible, get out of Orange County. There had to be life out there somewhere, and it was quickly passing me by.

My financial situation seemed to become more desperate with each passing month. I began to look for a job that would pay a higher salary. I managed to secure another secretarial position at a retirement community newspaper. It paid slightly more money and the work load was a lot less. I left the advertising agency, but I was not happy knowing that I would still be working for someone else. I simply was not cut out to be an employee.

One of the duties of my new job was to search through daily newspapers to see if there were any stories we could use in our paper. One morning, as I sat at my desk reading newspapers, a story caught my eye. A group of Native Americans had reclaimed the area known as Cleveland National Forest near San Juan Capistrano, California. In the article, they pointed out that the land had been taken from them illegally and they were now reclaiming it for their tribe.

I thought this was a fantastic idea. I immediately wrote a letter to the editor of the newspaper in support of the effort of the Native Americans. This was my first political move as a Native American, a Choctaw woman. My feet were now on a new path that I would walk for the rest of my life.

The weekend after my letter appeared in our local newspaper, I decided to drive to the Native American encampment. My plan was to stay the weekend and do whatever I could to be of help in the struggle.

It was dark when I drove down the dirt road leading into the camp. I could hear voices and laughter, and saw a large group of people sitting around a fire. As I parked my car, several of the men approached me. One of them was Clarence Lobo, chief of the Juaneño Band of Mission Indians.

When I identified myself, Chief Lobo welcomed me warmly. He was surprised that I was a young woman. He said that when he read my letter in the newspaper, he assumed it had been written by someone much older. He escorted me to the rest of the group and introduced me to everyone. For the first time in my life, I was surrounded by Native Americans who hugged me, thanked me for writing the letter, and welcomed me into their circle.

I looked around at the smiling faces and saw reflections of myself. I was no longer an outsider, someone who never quite fit in. I felt like the ugly duckling who had finally grown into a swan. I knew a fullness of spirit I had never before experienced. I was home at last.

CHAPTER TEN

The Road Becomes Harder

Give me a good way of living. May I . . .
safely reach the next year.

—Crow prayer

The hardest part of being a working mother was having to leave Pete every day. I was very fortunate that a close friend, Judianne, had offered to take care of him. I never worried a minute while Pete was in her loving, competent care.

However, when Judianne decided to go back to work, I was thrown into a state of panic. I had no idea where to even look for another sitter. I remembered reading an article in a newspaper about a private school that also had a preschool for children three years of age and older. Pete had just turned three so I thought maybe this would be a good place for him.

After further investigation, I learned that this was one of the most expensive schools in Orange County. The school was for "gifted children" who had to pass extensive testing before being admitted.

I knew that Pete, being an exceptionally bright child, could pass any test given to him. However, I would definitely have to find a second source of income to be able to afford the school's high tuition. Undaunted, I set up an interview with the school's director.

Pete was tested and passed with flying colors. Now all I had to do was come up with the money. I knew that with my limited work experience and skills, I was already earning the most I could earn as a secretary. But I firmly believed that I would find a way to make the extra money. Whenever I am faced with a problem, especially one that concerns the welfare of my children, I never think "*Can* I do this?" Rather, I think "*How* can I do this?"

I began avidly reading the help wanted columns of several different newspapers. The main problem I encountered was that mostly day jobs were offered. I already had a day job; I needed to find work that I could do at night.

One day while studying the classifieds, I noticed an ad for a barmaid. I had never thought about working in a bar; I had never even known anyone who worked in a bar. But it was a night job and surely anyone could pour beer. I called the phone number in the paper and went in for an interview.

The bar was in Anaheim, about a half hour's drive from where I was living. I was terrified as I walked through the door. I was sure the bar would be filled with men who would either rape or murder me, or possibly both.

The bar was dimly lit with music blaring from a jukebox. There were two pool tables at one end of the room where men stood holding bottles of beer and watching the players. The stools at the bar were completely full, as were the tables on the floor. All of the customers were men.

Five or six young women stood behind the bar. The floor behind the bar was raised so that the bar counter was only slightly higher than the women's knees. This way the barmaids were constantly in view, and they had to bend down over the bar to serve the beer. This was the first "girlie bar" in Orange County. (Actually, at that time, there may not have been anything like it in all of Southern California. However, within a year or two, these bars were everywhere and are still prevalent today.)

The man at the door asked if I had come to apply for work. I answered yes and he told me to go back into the restroom and try on one of the costumes. At that moment, I wanted desperately to go back out to my car and leave. I thought this bar was the worst place I had ever been in in all my life. But, remembering I had a child to support, I clenched my teeth and walked back to the women's restroom.

The costumes we were required to wear resembled Playboy Bunny costumes, only these had long sleeves. There was no way in the world I was going out of the restroom in that costume. I put my coat on over the costume, squared my shoulders, and walked out into the back room.

The same sleazy man I had talked to earlier was waiting for me. He took one look and said, "Take off the coat."

I pulled my coat tighter around me. "No," I said firmly.

The man reached out to open my coat. I held the coat tightly closed and backed up against the wall. At that moment I heard a firm voice order, "Leave her alone, Bill." I had been so concerned with keeping my coat around me that I was unaware another man had entered the room. The man walked forward and stood between me and the man who had been unsuccessfully trying to get me out of my coat.

"Hi, I'm Jack. I own this place." The man's voice was gentle. He was young, only a couple of years older than I. His dark hair was combed the same way that Elvis Presley wore his; in fact, he resembled Elvis quite a bit.

"Honey, would you take your coat off for me? I do need to see the costume," Jack asked in a soft casual voice that also reminded me of the way that Elvis spoke.

When I had been with Elvis, I always felt safe. At the time that I knew Elvis, he was a strong man, a man who could control any situation. In his presence I felt protected; nothing could ever hurt me. In those first few moments in the back room of that bar, I felt the same sense of security with Jack.

I slowly, timidly opened my coat. I stood before Jack holding the coat open wide. I still would not take it off.

Jack's smile broadened, "You have the job." In the meantime, Bill had moved around beside Jack and was openly leering at me. I wasn't sure if I wanted the job or not. I again thought of my small child.

"When do I start and what will my hours be?" I asked. "I work a full-time day job so I can only work nights and weekends."

"You can have whatever hours you want," Jack said, his eyes twinkling. His expression was one of obvious approval. "Would you like to start now?"

I quickly closed my coat. "No!"

Jack laughed. "Okay, honey. You can start whenever you want." He was obviously flirting with me, but in a clean, joking manner. On the other hand, Bill gave new meaning to the word "pervert."

Jack and I made out a work schedule, I changed back into my clothes, and he walked me out to my car. As I drove home, I was frightened at the thought of working in the bar, but I was also proud of myself. I would now have the money for Pete's private school tuition.

I will never forget my first night working there. I spent almost the entire evening standing behind the sink washing beer mugs. My knees were shaking so badly that I had to lean against the sink to keep from falling. The few customers that

I did serve all asked if it was my first night at work—my fear must have been clearly visible.

After working a couple of nights, I stopped being afraid of the customers, but I still couldn't stand being in a bar. More than anything else, I hated having to work in a smoke-filled room. I am an avid nonsmoker and most of the bar's customers smoked. When I got home at around three in the morning, my hair would be filled with smoke. It was too late to wash and dry my waist-length hair so I wore a shower cap to bed—otherwise, I would not have been able to sleep with that horrible odor.

During the four nights I worked at the bar each week, I earned more than twice the money I was making at the newspaper. I was able to pay Pete's tuition and bought a new condominium in a nice area. I managed to negotiate a good price for the condo because my unit was next to the playground area, and most people didn't want to hear children's voices all day. For me, it was perfect. Pete loved the playground, and I was able to closely supervise his play.

When my poor old car was finally beyond repair, I bought a used sports car. It was not very expensive and it was fun to drive. As much as I hated working in a bar, the extra income certainly did improve our lifestyle.

I especially hated the nights at work when Jack was not there. I felt completely vulnerable, missing the sense of security that his presence provided. Those nights, I kept telling myself over and over, "You can't go home. You have to do this. Pete has to be able to stay in school."

The other barmaids were always counting their tips, looking forward to buying new clothes, or going on a week-end trip. I counted my tips hoping to have enough money to pay for Pete's tuition, new shoes, and the babysitter.

The evenings when Jack left the bar, he went to other bars in the area to check out his competition. I had been working at the bar a little more than a week when he began asking me to go with him on some of these trips. We would have dinner and then go to the other bars. Jack and I also began spending time together during the few times I was not working at either the bar or the office. A couple of times we went to the horse races, but usually we would go to meetings with his lawyers or to look at nightclubs that were for sale. Jack's main focus in life was business, which I thoroughly enjoyed. He had a very creative mind and I learned many things by just watching him work. Everything Jack touched seemed to turn to money.

Whenever we would leave the bar, instead of using the money in his wallet, Jack would grab the money bag to take with us. I worried that we might get mugged, walking into restaurants carrying a full bag of money. One night, Jack left the bag in the booth at a restaurant and realizing his mistake when we were in the parking lot, ran back inside. Fortunately, the money bag was right where he had left it. By the time he got back to the car, I was in a state of panic. Jack just laughed; money was of secondary importance to him. First and foremost was the game of the business deal—Jack was truly a master at it.

I hated having to drive home alone after 2:00 A.M. Many times men would pull up beside me and start honking their horns trying to make me pull over. They seemed to think that because I was out alone late at night I was just waiting to be picked up.

One night when Jack walked me to my car after work, I noticed a customer sitting in his parked car. I told Jack that the man had been staring at me while I was working and I thought it was strange that he was now sitting alone in his car.

Jack went over to the man's car and asked him what he was doing. The man said that he thought I was very sexy in my costume and he wanted to talk to me. Jack became angry and told the man that I was his wife and that he should leave immediately. The man quickly left and Jack made me wait five or ten minutes before leaving to go home.

When I was on the freeway, I realized that the man I had seen outside of the bar was now in the car behind me. I started to go faster, but I couldn't lose him. He was still on my tail as I pulled off the freeway. My heart was pounding as I drove down a long city street toward home. My speedometer reached ninety, but the man's car was clearly visible in my rearview mirror.

As I approached a coffee shop, I was relieved to see my girlfriend's husband, Mike, in the parking lot talking to several other men. I hit my brakes and my tires screeched as I turned into the parking lot. As soon as my car stopped, I grabbed the keys, jumped out, and ran across the parking lot toward the men as fast as my four-inch heels would allow.

The men looked up, startled. I must have looked a sight. I was still wearing my costume, with the coat that covered it now flying open and my long hair streaming out behind me. The man who had been following me was now out of his car running after me.

When I reached my girlfriend's husband, I threw myself at him, wound my arms tightly around his neck, and refused to let go. As the man who had been chasing me approached, Mike managed to release himself from my tight grip.

"What do you want?" he asked the man in an angry voice.

"I just want to talk to her. Who is she to you?" the man answered in an equally angry voice.

"She's my goddamn wife, that's who she is," Mike yelled in a threatening manner.

As Mike and the other men started toward the man, he turned and ran back to his car, yelling over his shoulder, "Another husband?"

"What's he talking about?" Mike asked.

"Oh, my boss said I was his wife, too," I explained. We all laughed as Mike walked me back to my car.

I became very worried when Jack told me that he wanted to buy a large cocktail lounge close to Los Angeles and that he would have to sell the bar in Anaheim to do so. There was no way that I could pay my bills without the extra income from the bar. Jack had been encouraging me to move out of Orange County, but I kept resisting, explaining that I didn't want to take Pete out of the excellent school he was attending. Furthermore, I really didn't want to sell my condominium. Jack kept trying to change my mind, saying that he could see no opportunities whatsoever for me in Orange County.

He told me that if I would move to Los Angeles, I could work for him full time and make enough money so that I wouldn't have to work two jobs. It sounded very tempting, but I still did not have enough courage to make the move.

Much to my dismay, the bar sold quickly. I had already made up my mind that I would make the drive of more than an hour from my home to Jack's new club. Since that would mean getting even less sleep, I didn't know how I would survive. I already felt like a zombie most of the time.

Jack was very fair and actually fun to work for, so we didn't have the great turnover in barmaids that plagues most bars. However, one night we did have a new barmaid. She was a young woman who had just moved to Los Angeles from Canada. She worked a Saturday night shift and was supposed to come back and work the next day.

Many times, Jack, or the manager, Bill, had to work a late shift and then double back to work the next morning, so Jack kept a motel room close to the bar. Since the new girl lived in Los Angeles and would have to be back at work the next morning, Jack offered to let her use the motel room. Bill said he would go to the motel to make sure the desk clerk would let her in.

When I arrived at work Sunday evening, I noticed that the new girl was not there. I asked Jack what had happened and he said he didn't know; she had just disappeared. He thought maybe she decided that the drive from Los Angeles to Anaheim was too long, so she quit without bothering to notify him. He did think it was a little strange that she hadn't even come by to get her paycheck for working the night before. However, Jack had just picked up the signed contract for the sale of the bar so his thoughts quickly shifted back to the more important business at hand.

Jack said he would like me to read the sales contract and suggested that we go to dinner before I started working. I agreed, happy to get out of work for a while. Jack said that he was having car trouble so he was going to borrow Bill's car.

As we were leaving the bar, Jack mentioned to Bill that, when he went to the motel room in the afternoon to rest, the pillows were missing from the bed. He asked if Bill knew anything about it. Bill said he hadn't noticed but maybe the girl from Canada took them.

When we returned from dinner, Jack went back in to the bar to make sure everything was running smoothly. I sat alone in Bill's car with the overhead light on and read the contract. After about fifteen or twenty minutes, I went into the bar and started to work.

Six weeks later, Jack opened his new club near Los Angeles. The building was very large, with a cocktail lounge at one end and a huge double-looped beer bar and tables at the other. Bikini dancers performed on a raised platform a couple of feet above the tables. The bar was always full; sometimes, it was standing room only. All of the waitresses were required to wear bikinis and take turns dancing but Jack made an exception for me. I wore the same one-piece costume I had worn in Anaheim and I did not have to dance.

The other young women I worked with were all experienced barmaids and cocktail waitresses. Although I did not realize it, compared to the other women, I was still very innocent. They all jokingly referred to me as "the baby."

Some of the barmaids made more money in one night than a secretary could earn in a week. Therefore, it was rare for any of the women to ask for a night off. I remember when one young woman, Frankie, became pregnant, she kept right on working. Fortunately, she was carrying a small baby and she simply hung long, thick fringe from the top of her bikini to cover her stomach. When the baby was born, she took one night off from work and was back dancing the next night. She probably didn't have a choice; now she had a child to take care of.

Barbara, who was older than the rest of us, was tall with long, dyed, flaming red hair. I liked her very much, and realizing I needed help, she took me under her wing. I was definitely not a great cocktail waitress, but Barbara did her best to see that I got my share of tips.

It was very hard for me to say more than a few words to the customers; I simply didn't know what to talk about. Once in a while, I would find someone to discuss politics with, but other than that, I quietly went about my business. I think the customers understood that I had to force myself to be nice to them, which resulted in fewer tips. Although I never did make as much as the other waitresses, I was still earning a lot more than I had at the bar in Anaheim and I was even able to start saving money.

It seems that some of the most interesting events in my life have resulted from reading a newspaper or magazine article. I had recently read a story in a major magazine about Manuel Benítez, "El Cordobés," a new, young Spanish bullfighter who was creating a worldwide sensation. The article explained how he had grown up in absolute poverty but today was earning fabulous sums of money and was adored by the young women of Spain. Because of his haircut, he was referred to as "the blond Beatle of the bullring." Even though bullfighters are not usually well-known in America, El Cordobés had become an instant celebrity.

77

Not long after reading about El Cordobés, I saw a notice in a newspaper that he would soon be appearing in Tijuana, Mexico, just below the California border. I immediately decided to see him. I never even thought of trying to meet him; I simply wanted to see him.

When I arrived at the Plaza El Toreo in Tijuana, hundreds of people were pushing and shoving their way toward the ticket windows. I simply threw myself into their midst—there was no other way. Short of being trampled, nothing was going to keep me out of that plaza.

I was one of the lucky ones because I managed to get a ticket. If the plaza had been double in size, it could not have accommodated all the people wishing to see this exciting young man from Spain. Looking around the plaza, I could not help thinking that if this had been fifteen or twenty years earlier, the front row and boxes would have been filled with movie stars. In those days, Ava Gardner, Anthony Quinn, Lana Turner, Gilbert Roland, Brian Keith, and Sam Peckinpah could often be seen at the plaza.

El Cordobés lived up to his reputation. It was an afternoon of great excitement. The band played almost constantly. The plaza echoed with cries of "Olé!" Young American women threw their bras onto the sand. The club, where I was supposed to be at work, seemed very far away.

Walking back to my car, I cut through the parking lot of the La Sierra Motel and noticed a crowd of people and many policemen standing on the second-floor landing. I thought maybe someone had been murdered in one of the rooms.

I was suddenly approached by a short Mexican man who was speaking, very excitedly, in Spanish. I thought he was probably trying to sell me something and I told him in English that I did not speak Spanish. He responded in English, explaining that "his matador" had seen me walking through the parking lot and wanted to meet me. I glared at him in annoyance and ordered him out of my way. He refused to budge and stated emphatically that I must meet his matador. My patience was quickly waning. "Who is your matador?" I questioned, demandingly.

The man drew himself up to his full height of almost five feet. "El Cordobés," he claimed proudly, as he gestured toward the large crowd on the motel's walkway.

As I looked up at the building, I realized he was probably telling the truth. The police were there to control the crowd trying to get in to see the young bullfighting phenomenon. I quickly changed my mind and agreed to go with him.

With great difficulty, we managed to make our way through the crowd. A policeman helped us squeeze through the door that barely opened to admit us.

The motel room was filled with people, but somehow Manolo, as I came to call "El Cordobés," saw me as we entered. He broke into a smile as he quickly pushed his way through the crowd. He stood very close to me, put his hand on my arm, and spoke to me in Spanish. His words sounded wonderfully romantic, but I had absolutely no idea what he was talking about. I looked at him blankly and explained in English that I didn't speak Spanish. Manolo turned and spoke to a man standing next to him who then conveyed to me that Manolo wanted me to stay and have dinner with him. As I accepted his invitation, I became aware that everyone in the room was staring at me. I felt very uncomfortable.

The room was so crowded that it was hard to move. I finally found a place to sit on a bed in front of the windows while a reporter interviewed Manolo. While he was still being interviewed, waiters brought in trays piled high with chicken dinners. Before I could even begin to eat, I heard a metallic ripping sound that turned out to be the window screen being torn out of its frame. The window was forced open as a horde of Manolo's fans pushed their way through the opening and into the room.

Unfortunately, I was sitting on the bed right beneath the window. I was instantly knocked flat onto the bed. The chicken dinner I had been holding was now upside down on my chest, while many pairs of high-heeled shoes crushed me onto the mattress. Policemen were yelling; it was absolute pandemonium.

When all the feet finally passed over me, I managed to sit back up and was horrified to see that my clothes were covered with chicken, vegetables, and rice. I looked across the room to see Manolo standing up on the other bed, his shoulders pressed against the wall. Several young women were grabbing at him and trying to kiss him. They had already ripped his clothes off down to his undershorts, each wanting to take home a piece of his clothing as a souvenir. Fortunately, policemen managed to reach his determined fans and quickly dragged them screaming and yelling out of the room. At that point, I wasn't sure that dating superstars was such a good idea.

Later, Manolo and I were able to talk to each other with the help of a bilingual friend. He asked if I would accompany him to a town where he would be fighting the next day. I explained that it was not possible but promised to see him the next time he was in Tijuana.

During the next year or two, I saw Manolo whenever he was in Mexico. I enjoyed the time I spent with him and life was very exciting, but there were also problems. Even though I had begun to learn Spanish, verbal communication was still difficult. The worst problem, however, was security. Many women, jealous of my relationship with Manolo, had made threats against me. Whenever I was with him in Mexico, I couldn't safely go anywhere alone. But, all in all, it was an interesting time in my life.

About three months after Jack sold the bar in Anaheim, I was reading the morning paper when I noticed a terrible story on the front page. A woman's body had been discovered in the trunk of a car and a man had been arrested for her murder. The man's name was given in the article, but I didn't immediately recognize it.

About an hour later, the phone rang. I answered to hear Jack's concerned voice. "Baby, are you all right?"

"Yes, why?" I asked, puzzled at his question.

"Have the police been there yet?" Jack asked. Now he had my full attention.

"No!" I practically yelled. "Why would the police be here?"

"Did you read about the trunk murder?" he asked.

"Yes," I replied, thinking back to the article. All of a sudden, I remembered that the man accused of the murder was named Bill. "Oh, my God!" I screamed. "Was that Bill?"

"Yeah, it was," Jack sighed. "I can't believe it. We've been friends since high school. All I could think of when I found out was that sometimes he used to walk you out to your car."

Then I remembered Jack had asked if the police had been at my house. "Why do the police want to talk to me?"

"Well, you remember the night we borrowed Bill's car? He killed her the night before and when we were in the car, her body was in the trunk."

Now I was screaming. "You mean while I was sitting alone in the car reading that contract, she was in the trunk?"

"Yes, baby, I'm afraid so."

Jack said that he would call the police to see if I could go to the Anaheim station to talk to them rather than have them come to my house. I was relieved when he called back, saying that they had agreed to meet with me at the station.

My visit with the officers in Anaheim was a most unpleasant experience. The policemen treated me as if I were personally responsible for the young woman's death. They tried to make me look at pictures of the body taken after it had been in the trunk of the car for three months. I refused.

They grilled me intensely on my relationship with Jack. I failed to see any connection. They seemed to believe that since I was a barmaid and Jack owned the bar, our relationship must be quite perverse. Nothing could have been further from the truth. Jack was a very decent man and we cared very much for each other.

That night I met Jack for dinner, and he filled me in on the horrible details of the murder. When Bill had gone to the motel with the barmaid, he had insisted on going into the room with her. He made sexual advances toward her, which she rebuffed. She explained that she had undergone an abortion shortly before leaving Canada and was terrified of becoming pregnant again. Bill paid no attention to her pleas, and as his advances became stronger, she began to fight.

Bill told Jack that he simply lost control and strangled her. He said that he strangled her so hard that blood poured from her mouth and stained the pillows on the bed. He put her body, her purse, and the pillows into the trunk of his car. (That explained why the pillows were missing when Jack went to the room the next day.)

Bill told Jack that he drove around with her body in the trunk of his car for three months. He made several trips to the desert to dump the body, but each time cars kept driving by and he was afraid he would be seen.

On Father's Day, Bill was at his parents' house. When his father walked by Bill's car, he noticed a strong, putrid odor coming from the trunk of the car. He asked his son about it, but Bill was very vague, saying that he thought a cat had crawled into the trunk and died.

His father kept insisting that the trunk would have to be cleaned out. Bill kept saying he'd do it later; finally, his father took the keys and opened the trunk. At first it was not clear if what was in the trunk was animal or human. Apparently, in the heat of the trunk, the body had become so severely bloated that it exploded, leaving decomposed pieces of flesh throughout the trunk. This was what had been displayed in the photographs that the police tried to make me view.

As Bill's father stared into the trunk, his disgust turned to horror as he noticed a woman's purse. He then realized that the carnage in the trunk was human. Bill confessed to the murder and his father called the police. He went to trial, was sentenced, and served about five years in prison. Many times I have wondered if the short sentence was due to the fact that the innocent victim was a barmaid who recently had an abortion.

The only real problem with working in the new bar was the long drive to and from work. By the time I started home after two in the morning, I would be so tired that I could hardly keep my eyes open. Driving down the freeway, I would get what is called "truck driver's vision." I guess the name comes from the problems truck drivers have when they have to drive for many hours without any rest. While driving, I would hallucinate and think that there was a huge truck or moving van stopped in front of me. I would slam on the brakes and then I would see that there was nothing in the road. It is a miracle that I was never rear-ended by another car.

At least a couple of times each night, I would fall asleep and my car would drift off of the asphalt and up into the ivy embankment at the side of the freeway. I would instantly wake up, climb out of the car, and do jumping jacks at the side of the freeway, trying to make myself stay awake. Unfortunately, as soon as I was behind the wheel again, my sleepiness would return.

One night as I was driving, I suddenly realized I was passing through Laguna Hills. I was still on the freeway, but I had passed the turnoff to my house at least a half-hour earlier. I must have been asleep or at least totally out of touch with my surroundings. I will never know for sure how my car managed to stay on the road. Even though there was traffic on the freeways night and day, somehow I was able to keep driving and not hit any other cars.

Another night when I was late coming home, my babysitter came out to the garage to see if my car was there. She found me slumped over the steering wheel sound asleep.

These were very hard times and they continued that way for two more years. I worked forty hours a week in the office and Thursday through Sunday nights at the bar. I wore three- or four-inch heels day and night. At night, I walked nonstop on a cement floor carrying trays of drinks.

When I finally did get home, during the three hours that I was in bed, I had to prop my legs up on pillows to try to relieve the shooting pains that ran through my feet and legs. Life was hard, but I knew I had to keep going. My first prayer every morning was to ask for the strength to take care of my child.

Pete's father still came by to see us whenever he had time, which wasn't very often. He had finally saved enough money to open a beer bar a few miles from the ocean. It was a great success as the beach crowd packed in nightly, resulting in standing room only. After receiving several citations for exceeding the legal room occupancy, he opened another bar in Santa Ana about 10 miles away. The second bar was as successful as the first, leaving very little time for anything other than work.

I worried constantly that I had so little time to spend with my son. We occasionally did manage to get away to Disneyland, the beach, or a park, but it seemed that most of my waking hours were spent working to support us.

Life became easier when Jack bought an entertainment newspaper in Hollywood. I quit my office job and went to work for Jack. I still worked at the club, but Jack arranged my hours so that I was able to make enough money without working double shifts as I had done for the past two years.

The office in Hollywood was crazy. Jack was in partnership with another man who had strange women, including strippers, running in and out of the office. Gypsy Boots visited us daily, handing out his week-old fruit. Gypsy was an older man with long, straggly hair and an unkempt beard. He was Hollywood's own "nature boy" who would burst into our office with a gaggle of scantily dressed girls following behind and throw fruit wildly about the room. I wondered if ours was a typical Hollywood office.

Jack kept insisting that since I was now working in Hollywood it would be much easier for me if I moved into town. I knew he was right, but I still wasn't ready to make such a drastic change. Even though I disliked living in Orange County, I was happy with my condominium and Pete was doing very well in his private school. Hollywood would just have to wait.

CHAPTER ELEVEN

A Time for Change

Time rolls on without ceasing. The winter passes quickly away, and the summer is here again . . .

—Methoataske, Muskogee Creek, mother of Tecumseh, 1770s

I had been working in Hollywood only a few months when Jack announced that he was selling the newspaper and closing the office. He had recently opened a second club featuring live bands that played to a full house every night. Between running two successful nightclubs, he simply did not have time left for a newspaper that was only turning a marginal profit.

Jack tried to discourage me from looking for daytime employment, assuring me that I would make enough money working in his clubs. I welcomed the thought of only working nights, but I couldn't overcome my fear of poverty. For a while, at least, I felt it necessary to work two jobs.

The only other person in Jack's office whom I considered relatively sane was Lisa, a young woman from Austria. She had been living in the United States for only two years. Jack tried to keep Lisa on the phones as much as possible, believing her charming accent gave the office a little class.

Lisa's short dark hair framed a pixieish face. She always wore the latest European fashions, which looked very stylish on her slender frame. Lisa was educated and intelligent, and I was surprised that she was willing to work in our extremely unorthodox office.

During the months we worked in the Hollywood office, Lisa and I became friends. With the office now closing, both of us worried about finding other jobs. We hated to give up the fun we had working together and the totally free, if somewhat crazy, work environment. However, before either of us found new jobs, once again, fate intervened.

Lisa and I were in my car driving down Sunset Boulevard when we were rear-ended at a red light. Fortunately, the man who hit us was insured and we decided to use the insurance money to open a boutique.

While waiting for the settlement to come in, Lisa worked at an office in Hollywood. I took a job at a hofbrau across from the Costa Mesa Country Club, which was about 15 minutes from my condominium. The hofbrau served good lunches, and many men from the country club came in to eat after playing golf. Another large group of men from a nearby aerospace plant stopped by for lunch almost daily.

Working at the hofbrau was a real shock after working so long for Jack. The bar was owned by a young couple and one of them was always on the premises. The husband was very nice and easy to work for, but the wife was a real barracuda. I have found this situation to be true in most bars that are owned and operated by married couples.

I think her real problem was jealousy. The costumes we were required to wear were very flattering. The skirts just covered our hips and the blouses were very low-cut with large, short, puffy sleeves. At our waist, we wore wide, black, laced cummerbunds. I guess I looked better in my costume than she did because the customers paid a lot of attention to me, which made her furious.

She was actually an attractive young woman with strawberry blond hair, blue eyes, and a nice figure. However, she truly gave new meaning to the word "bitch." She treated the waitresses terribly, except for one young woman who was the least attractive of us all. She should have realized that pretty waitresses were good for business, but I think her insecurity interfered with her reasoning.

I made up my mind to ignore her and do my best to keep my job until Lisa and I could open our boutique. I was still working weekends for Jack, which was a wonderful relief from my work at the hofbrau. It was only the long drive to and from Los Angeles that made things difficult. However, I still cared for Jack and felt secure and sheltered while working for him.

Shortly after I began my job at the hofbrau, my sports car died; reviving it was hopeless. In desperation, I bought a car for twenty-five dollars. It was very old and barely ran, and I was sure it would fall apart any minute. I bought a can of yellow house paint and painted the car bright yellow with flowers all over it and eyelashes around the headlights. I christened her "Maisie the Daisy." After all, this was the '60s and the height of love-ins and flower children.

The only problem with driving Maisie was having to pick Pete up at the exclusive private school he was still attending. The other parents drove Jaguars, Mercedes, or Lincolns. Each day I parked almost a block from the school and walked the rest of the way.

Pete was doing very well in school. Since he was three years old, he not only learned to read and write in English but also learned to speak some French. As busy as my schedule was, I never missed a parents' meeting or open house. Of all the mothers who picked their children up after school, I was the only one who daily talked to the teacher to inquire about my child's progress.

During the time I worked at the hofbrau, I became friends with two of our customers. This was a new experience because at Jack's "girlie" bars I hadn't even viewed the customers as human beings. The hofbrau was only open during daytime hours and was more of a restaurant than a bar.

William, one of the men from the aerospace plant, came in frequently for lunch. He was a tall, attractive man in his late thirties and painfully shy around women. Unless he was ordering lunch, he never talked to me, but when he thought I wasn't looking, I often caught him staring at me. I was not surprised when his friends told me that, although he had been happily married for years, he had developed a crush on me.

Poor William. His crush quickly became a great source of entertainment for his friends. I knew they teased him about me because many times his face would be bright red from embarrassment. I made matters worse by flirting with him relentlessly.

To have money to keep the jukebox playing, the waitresses were required to play a game with the customers. We carried a bottle filled with numbered balls. We shook the bottle and then dropped a ball into the hand of each customer. The customer who received number seven or eleven had to give the waitress a couple of quarters for the jukebox.

William's friends and I plotted a new version of the game to play a joke on William. I carried the bottle and loudly announced to the customers that we were going to play for jukebox money. Whoever got the seven had to give two quarters, whoever got the eleven had to give two quarters, and whoever got the five got a kiss from the barmaid.

I kept the five ball in my palm and dropped the rest of the balls out of the bottle and into the waiting hands of William's friends and other customers. I approached William last, quietly dropping the five ball back into the bottle for him to draw.

I collected the quarters for the jukebox and then began calling out for the five ball. No one responded. I called out again and William barely whispered, "I have it." Of course, all of his friends immediately began giving catcalls and whistles. I ran over, told William what a rascal he was, and then leaned over the bar and gave him a big kiss. All of his friends applauded.

I thought the poor man would die. His face was crimson. His friends kept teasing him as I calmly returned to work. But William was a married man. Although that was the one and only time I ever kissed him, for the next couple of years, he did become an important part of my life.

William was kind and conscientious—a truly good man. I believe he thought he was in love with me, and I know it was a source of pain for him. He was not a man who would find it easy to betray his marriage vows.

We began going to dinner once a week. I felt guilty when William told me that he hid our dinner money under the floor mat of his car; he was so afraid that his wife would find out. He said that never, in all his years of marriage, had he even thought of being unfaithful. I tried to assure him that a platonic friendship was no cause for guilt.

Having William for a friend was almost like having a part-time husband. He worked on my car, fixed my garbage disposal when it frequently jammed, and occasionally helped me out with small financial matters.

Once William asked if he could kiss me. I refused, explaining that I would not let him do something he would one day regret. I would not allow him to be unfaithful to his wife. He said that he had already been unfaithful in his heart and that was just as bad. I still refused to let our relationship go any further; I believe I made the right decision. William is one of the few totally good individuals I have ever known. I still treasure the time I spent with him.

The other customer I became friends with was the exact opposite of William. He was a very elderly man and one of the richest and most powerful attorneys in the state. When I met Jacob, I thought he was a dear little old man. I viewed him as a grandfather. I thought he was kind, thoughtful, and generous, and I cared about him.

Jacob came into the hofbrau once or twice a week after golfing at the country club. I enjoyed talking to such a brilliant and worldly man, and I was thrilled by the extravagant tips he gave me. He talked to me about going to college, pursuing a career, or opening a business of my own. I was glad that someone other than myself understood that my current line of work was only temporary and could appreciate my dreams of a better lifestyle.

Before Christmas, Jacob gave me enough money to buy many wonderful gifts for Pete, and he presented me with a good, reliable used car. It was the first Christmas I had spent as an adult that had not been a financial struggle. I was happy beyond belief.

I still thought of Jacob as an adopted grandfather. When I talked to my grandmother about him, she also thought he was wonderful. My grandfather didn't trust him for a minute. But I could not believe that a man of Jacob's age could have anything on his mind except friendship. I was very wrong.

One day, as Jacob was driving me back from lunch in his big new Cadillac, he calmly asked, "When are you going to let me love you?"

At first I thought I must have misunderstood him. This was a very elderly man. His hands had liver spots and were slightly palsied. He wore a hearing aid that he turned down whenever he was around noise. I sincerely doubt that he could have done anything sexual if his life depended on it.

I could only gasp, "But I do love you. I think of you just like a grandfather."

I'm sure that was not what he wanted to hear, but still he didn't give up. "No, I mean I'd like to make love to you."

I felt sick. I cared about this man, but I viewed his proposal as something almost incestuous. I'm sure he saw the

91

horror in my face as I muttered that he was married and for him to be unfaithful to his wife was a sin against the church. (I didn't specify which church.) At that point I would have said anything.

Jacob didn't give up. He told me that before we became intimate he would deposit money into an account in my name. It would be enough so that I could buy a business of my choice and also put Pete through college. He was talking a lot of money. He said he would give me time to think it over.

I was in shock. I knew I would die before I let him touch me, but I felt I would let Pete down if I did not accept the money. Life was a struggle. I worked two jobs, scrambled for every penny, and was always broke. I knew I should take Jacob up on his offer, but I couldn't bring myself to do it.

I tried to force myself. I even thought of being hypnotized. But the thought of what would happen afterward always stopped me. I simply couldn't do it. I talked to Jacob and explained that I could never think of being with a married man, but that I really cared about him and hoped that our friendship could continue as before. Obviously, he didn't feel the same way. Jacob stopped coming to the hofbrau, and I never saw him again.

In addition to working weekdays at the hofbrau and weekends for Jack, I was also spending many hours with Lisa, trying to find a location, fixtures, and inventory for our boutique. When the time I was able to spend with Pete each day became shorter and shorter, I knew I had to make a change. Though losing the extra income would be very difficult, I made the decision to quit working for Jack.

As always, Jack was understanding and supportive, and assured me if I ever needed anything he would always be there for me. We continued to see each other occasionally, but once again, distance became the destroying factor in the relationship. Jack was working long hours running two very successful clubs. I juggled my schedule around working at the hofbrau, trying to get ready to open a boutique, and still managing to find time to spend with my six-year-old son.

I found being apart from Jack difficult. Working for him had helped me financially, and I had turned to him for emotional support as well. Jack was one of the few individuals I have known in my life who seemed to know all the right answers. He was strong and capable and when I was with him I felt totally protected and secure. It was a wonderful feeling because I usually was the one everyone else turned to for support.

Jack went on to become one of the most successful club owners in the country. He is very well known and has been featured in many newspaper and magazine articles. Although our relationship never resumed the intimacy we had once known, in later years whenever our paths crossed, there was still a feeling of warmth and caring between us.

Thankfully, it wasn't long after I stopped working for Jack that the insurance money came in and Lisa and I opened a boutique in Costa Mesa, California. Our shop carried the latest hip fashions for men and women. Our walls were covered with psychedelic and rock group posters, and we had a large back room where customers could sit, relax, and talk while we served espresso or cappuccino. Incense burned constantly and music blared. It was the late '60s and everything was love, music, and flowers. We called our store "The Psyche Shoppe."

Our presence in staid Orange County did not go unnoticed. We attended every "love-in" within driving distance. The county newspaper ran a story about our shop with the heading, "Hippies Invade Orange County." Our shop was always full of beautiful, long-haired, young people. The police visited us at least once a day.

Lisa and I were in our element. We found a great dressmaker in Newport Beach, only ten minutes from our store. We could show Jeanne a picture of a dress from a top fashion magazine and she could copy it exactly within a day or two.

I'm not sure this was ethical, or even legal, but Lisa and I were certainly well-dressed. We had incredibly short skirts and dresses, and the most outrageous jewelry and hair ornaments. To make skirts required less than a half of a yard of material, and the dresses we sold could better be described as long blouses.

With the money left over from investing in The Psyche Shoppe, Lisa put a down payment on a new car, and I made summer reservations for a very low-priced trip to Europe. I felt that I had worked exceptionally hard for five years with no time off, and I deserved a vacation. My cousin, Jennifer, agreed to take care of Pete for me while I was out of the country.

Two months before I left for Europe, I met a beautiful, long-haired, young man named Jim. He was a lot younger than I and our affair was considered quite scandalous. Nonetheless, he was one of the great loves of my life.

Shortly before I was scheduled to leave for Europe, Lisa and I decided to sell our inventory and close the boutique. The store was making far less money than we had expected and Lisa knew she could make more money working in an office in Los Angeles. I wasn't quite sure what I would do when I returned from Europe, but I knew I could always get a job in a nightclub or go back to work for Jack.

Because of Jim, I almost cancelled my trip to Europe. I'm still surprised I didn't. I was madly in love with him, but I refused to cancel my trip. Looking back, I realize that I was being guided along a predestined pathway. I had to move on. If I had not gone to Europe, my life might have been very different.

At the airport I cried so hard I could barely get on the plane. Jim and I promised undying love and vowed that nothing would ever part us again when I returned in ten weeks.

I enjoyed Europe, but it was a very long trip. I saw the bullfighter, El Cordobés, again briefly in Spain, but my interest had waned considerably. I spent a week in Pamplona during the running of the bulls. That was the highlight of my trip. I was in Paris several times. I loved the city and spent three days in the Louvre. I met many people and saw a lot of interesting places, but I had never been away from my son before and I missed him terribly. I was glad to get on the plane to fly back to the United States.

When I returned, Jim had moved to the small mountain community of Idyllwild and was living with his older sister and some of her friends. At first, I was devastated. I still loved Jim and couldn't bear to think of us no longer living together. However, after spending some time with him in the mountains, I realized that our lifestyles were very different.

Jim's life was one party after another, while my time was filled with hard work and trying to raise a son. I knew that although I deeply loved him, there could be no real future for us. Even though I wanted to keep seeing him as often as possible, I could also feel something pulling me in another direction. I sensed there was something I had to do, some destiny yet to be fulfilled.

With Jim in Idyllwild, I was basically "single" once again, but I had no interest in dating. Whenever a man asked me out I would think of Jim and turn him down. I still wasn't ready to let go of the incredible love we had shared.

Pete still called regularly, and occasionally came by to visit with our son. Now that Jim was gone, Pete's calls became more frequent. One evening he called and said he was close by and asked if he could come over. I said yes, thinking he wanted to visit with little Pete. However, when he arrived, I realized I was the one he wanted to be with. When our son was in bed, he put his arms around me and drew me to him. I didn't make any attempt to stop him, but when he kissed me I thought of Jim and started to cry. Pete angrily left, telling me that when I got over "that kid" to give him a call. Over the next two or three years, as Jim continued to move in and out of my life, several other men would utter the same complaint.

I didn't want to take Pete away from his father, but I knew there was nothing for me in Orange County. It was time to leave.

Two months after I returned from Europe, I leased out the condo and moved to Los Angeles.

CHAPTER TWELVE

Freedom

Let me be . . . free to follow the religion of my
fathers, free to talk and think
and act for myself . . .

—Chief Joseph, Nez Perce, 1880s

*W*hen I moved to Los Angeles from Orange County I felt as if I had been released from prison. I could breathe and move, and no one was watching my every action. The feeling of freedom was euphoric.

Pete and I moved into a nice large fourplex in the mid-Wilshire section of Los Angeles, less than five minutes from Beverly Hills. We immediately became close friends with everyone in the building. Barbara, whose son Dimitri was a couple of years younger than Pete, had the apartment across the hall. Diane and Eric lived downstairs with their baby girl, Krista. In the other downstairs unit was Mary, a lovely, older professional woman. She was raising her niece, Helen, who attended art school. Everyone in the building was intelligent, educated, and fun. I considered myself very lucky.

I found a live-in babysitter who occupied a small room next to the kitchen. Buena worked days at a major department store but was home with Pete in the evenings when I worked. I enrolled Pete in a very nice elementary school a few blocks from our apartment. Every day, I would drag myself out of bed, fix Pete's breakfast, and drive him to school. Then I would come back home and sleep a while longer because I worked until two every morning and never got to sleep before 4:00 A.M. After school, I picked Pete up and had time to supervise his homework and cook his dinner before I left for work.

The only downside about leaving Orange County was moving away from my grandparents and Pete's father. Mama and Daddy especially hated to see us go because Pete, being the first boy in my grandmother's family in five generations, was truly the light of their lives. While Pete and I managed to see them at least once or twice a month, Pete saw very little of his father. A year before we moved, Pete had sold the bars and started law school, so his time was almost completely devoted to his studies. I suffered from feelings of guilt because I had not been able to provide my son with a stable two-parent home. I realized several years earlier that Pete's father and I would never be able to live together. In many ways we were very different, but in others we were exactly alike. When we were together, I always downplayed our differences, but I knew if we were living together, the problems would surface. The bottom line was we were two strong, hard-headed individuals and if we had to be together every day, we would soon begin to hate each other. I felt, even though it meant depriving Pete of spending much time with his father, it was better to keep things as they were so that his parents would at least continue to care for each other.

Fortunately, my new life was so busy I didn't have much time to worry about Pete's father. From all over the country, young people were flocking to Hollywood. Every night, the

Sunset Strip was so crowded that you could hardly walk. Major bands were playing at The Whisky a Go Go or at The Cheetah in Santa Monica. New bands were cropping up almost daily and playing the smaller clubs. Everyone was doing something. Everyone had a dream. The air was filled with energy, magic, and excitement.

I volunteered to work a couple of afternoons a week at The Free Clinic, which served as a medical center for hippies and lesser-known musicians. It seemed that most of our patients had either a bad cold, venereal disease, or both.

I also helped with the rock concerts given to benefit the clinic. I remember one particular concert at The Cheetah by the Santa Monica Pier. The Grass Roots was one of the major bands appearing that night. Warren Entner was the lead singer and I had made up my mind to meet him. I wasn't quite sure how I would accomplish this, but I had enough faith in myself to know I would come up with something.

I thought back to my sophomore year in high school when I had a crush on a young singer named Chuck Hicks. He appeared on a weekly television show and I pestered my grandfather until he agreed to drive me to the large stadium where the program was taped. The show was filmed before a live audience that had been composed mostly of families until Chuck Hicks joined the production. Now every week in front of the stage were 50 to 100 screaming teenage girls. I made up my mind *not* to be one of those girls.

I convinced Jennifer to go with me. I told her it would be a very exciting evening—one she definitely would not want to miss. Jennifer was not so sure. But, as always, whenever I really needed my cousin, she was always there for me. She and I spent the rest of the week deciding what I should wear. We finally decided on a skin tight, red jersey dress and black spike-heeled shoes. I was sure I would look very sexy and sophisticated and Chuck Hicks would instantly fall madly in love with me. (Actually, I think I looked more like Vampira in red. I was not yet fifteen years old.)

I was reminded of the year before when at thirteen Jennifer and I had gone on vacation to Reno, Nevada, with my grandparents and GoGo. Jennifer and I had decided we were going out alone on the town. We put on a lot of makeup and tight, very grown-up dresses and managed to get served in a cocktail lounge. The only thing we knew to order was a martini—very dry. It almost killed me, but I forced myself to drink it. At first, Jennifer refused to drink the bitter cocktail, but I reminded her, through clenched teeth, that if she didn't finish every last drop, I would beat her up. Remembering how I used to fight with her when we were little girls, she dutifully finished her martini.

Jennifer and I thought we were quite a success that evening. All the men in the lounge kept wanting to dance with us and we believed they thought we were gorgeous. Looking back at how we were dressed at such a young age, I'm sure they thought we were hookers.

When we left the lounge we bumped right into GoGo. She had been there watching us the entire evening. We never could fool GoGo. She always said, "Don't ever think you can trick me. Whatever you're planning on doing, I've already done it." She was right.

My grandfather was less than happy when he left Jennifer and me at the television show to see Chuck Hicks. He told us not to talk to anyone, and he would be waiting outside when it was over. Once we were inside, I managed to push myself through the crowd, dragging Jennifer with me. We ended up in front of center stage. When Chuck started to sing, he looked out at a sea of screaming fans and one fourteen-year-old in a tight red dress standing perfectly still and giving him the sexiest look she could manage. He definitely took notice. The rest of the evening, whenever he sang, he leaned over the railing and sang directly to me. I remained perfectly still trying to appear completely composed, but my heart was pounding.

I continued going to see him and we eventually did go out a couple of times. But he was sixteen and, at least locally, a teenage idol, and I simply was not willing to go as far as he wanted. I'm sure he moved on to teenage groupies who, sadly, would do anything to please their idol.

Now, determined to meet Warren Entner, I decided what had worked with Chuck Hicks should also work with Warren. At least I hoped it would. Halfway through the group's last song, I positioned myself directly in front of the stage. I was wearing a very, very short white dress and high spiked heels. Warren noticed me immediately. Just as the song was ending, I turned and started walking away through the crowd. My plan worked. Warren dropped his guitar, jumped over the stage railing, and ran after me. He grabbed my arm, introduced himself, and asked me to go to breakfast with him.

I, of course, accepted. He followed me in his car to a restaurant and then back to my apartment. He later seemed frustrated when I refused to have sex with him. He kept reminding me that this was the age of free love, and I kept remembering all of those free-love cases that we treated daily at the clinic. Nonetheless, it was an interesting evening.

Not long after my Warren Entner escapade, I got a small part in a play. It wasn't scheduled to run long, but it was fun. When it ended, someone suggested that I try out for a part in a play that was projected to be a major long-running production. Thinking that acting in a play would be much more fun than working in a club, I went to the audition. This was the final audition and since I didn't know much about acting, my hopes were not high. An accomplished actress was returning for the third time to try out for the same part, and everyone believed she would definitely be chosen.

The play was about a cruel nurse in a mental hospital who eventually gets raped by an African American patient. The play had violence, nudity, and profanity—all the ingredients to make it a long-running success.

At the audition, I really got into it; I turned into a mad, raving lunatic, and got the part. I was more surprised than anyone. It was great. We were written up in *Variety* and soon began rehearsing. Then the director got the Hong Kong flu and lost all of his backing; that was the end of my acting career.

I soon recovered from my disappointment over the play. Life was too busy to allow me to remain depressed for long. I partied frequently with a bunch of wild, crazy, and beautifully dressed young people. We were invited everywhere. We always had guest passes for rock concerts and other events. Most weeknights we went to The Whisky a Go Go, but never on the weekends when it was full of tourists. We thought that would be just too, too tacky.

Frank Zappa had a big log cabin in Laurel Canyon and we visited there quite often. Actually, Mr. Zappa was a very levelheaded business man who kept his refrigerator locked. So much for the free spirit of the love generation.

We occasionally visited Vito, a more-than-crazy, middle-aged individual who drove his even crazier dance group around in a very old van. A lot of people stayed at Vito's house, including an artist whose prized exhibit was a line of framed used Kotex.

I met Jimi Hendrix several times and even went to a party one night at his house in one of the canyons. When I walked in, he was sitting in front of the fireplace, surrounded by three young blondes. He looked up when I came in and motioned for me to come over to him. I smiled, shook my head, and left. He looked like he had his hands full with the blondes.

Paul McCartney followed me out of one party trying to get me to stay. I wasn't interested and left. With all the excitement going on in Hollywood at the time, I was becoming very blasé. Even though I had quickly become used to the free passes to all events, invitations to parties with rock groups, and driving around in limousines, I still had one hard and fast rule: I never asked to be introduced to a rock or movie star and under no circumstances would I ever ask for an autograph.

I saw how groupies were treated and I had heard stars laughing about them. I knew one woman, Wesley, who was only twenty-one years old and went to bed with a different band member almost every night of the week. The men she met usually played in unknown bands that were featured in the small clubs along the Sunset Strip. Ninety-five percent of the time I knew Wesley, she had a venereal disease. I had met her when I was volunteering at The Free Clinic and in the year or so that I knew her, I believe she had every venereal disease known to man, with the exception of syphilis. It was impossible for me to understand how she could degrade herself by chasing after men who would only use her for an hour or so and then leave. Wesley was a very nice, intelligent young woman and she deserved so much more than she was getting out of life. She finally stopped picking up men when she had a baby and went back to school. She was never sure who the baby's father was.

I could see that some groupies seemed to enjoy their lifestyle, but I thought their lives were tragic. Even though I missed meeting some interesting stars, I never broke my rule and only went out with men who approached me first.

During all this insanity, Jim was still in my life. He was traveling most of the time, but every so often he managed to find his way to Los Angeles. When I would come home and find a sleeping bag rolled up inside of my doorway, I knew he was back.

Since life had become so much fun, work seemed worse than ever. After working at several clubs on the Strip, and not making much money, I took a job at a beer bar in Los Angeles. I hated the bar and the owner, Rick, but I made good money and the customers never bothered me.

While part of my life seemed to be all fun, there was another part that was quite serious. Soon after I arrived in

Hollywood, I became part of a Native American political group. We worked very hard trying to correct some of the many injustices that indigenous people have suffered over the past 500 years.

Although my days and nights were very busy, I had the feeling I was just treading water. I believed there was a definite purpose to my life. I simply did not yet know what it was.

CHAPTER THIRTEEN

Mexico

*I lie down with you, I rise up with you, in
my dreams you are with me.*

—Aztec love song

*E*ven though my life in Hollywood was very exciting, I
still visited Mexico whenever possible. It was during one of
these visits that I met a bullfighter who would play an important part in the changes that were about to come into my
life.

One afternoon, I was in Tijuana with a man who I was
occasionally dating. We were seated at the bullring when a
young new bullfighter walked out onto the sand. He was
dressed in light blue and had the most incredible face I had
ever seen. I tried not to react, but I'm sure I looked like a
cat staring at a canary. My date, Richard, even commented,
"My God, that kid's good looking."

I tried to pretend I hadn't noticed. I knew this young
man was scheduled to appear again in Tijuana; I planned to
be there also, but definitely without Richard.

A few weeks later, with my friend Lisa in tow, I headed for the border determined to meet the gorgeous young bullfighter. Lisa tried to convince me that I was crazy and that I'd never even get near him. He was an idol in Mexico and a million girls were always running after him. I flippantly told Lisa that I had no intention of chasing him—I planned to have him chase after me. In reality, I could only think of that perfect face I had seen a few weeks earlier. I was obsessed. I knew that nothing could keep me out of Mexico and no one would stop me from meeting this incredibly handsome young man.

Later that afternoon, Lisa and I were standing with a crowd of people outside of the small chapel at the bullring. The young bullfighter, Francisco, was nowhere to be seen, but I did notice one of his helpers standing near the door to the chapel. I moved closer to him and asked him for the time, which he gave me and then he asked my name. When I told him, I heard a voice behind me repeat my name. I turned and looked into Francisco's eyes. He took my hand and repeated my name again. All I could do was wish him luck. "Suerte, matador," I said, my eyes never leaving his. He squeezed my hand before turning and walking into the plaza. I had no doubt that I would see him again that night.

At that time, almost all of the bullfighters stayed at the venerable old hotel, Caesar's, in downtown Tijuana. The run-down building had definitely seen better days, but there was still a charm and an air of excitement upon entering the lobby. In that hotel, everyone knew what everyone else was doing. It was impossible to keep a secret. In front of the hotel were tables where drinks were served, and people sitting there were able to watch anyone who entered or left. In order to avoid the crowd in front of the hotel, it was possible to enter the lobby through the gift shop. However, there was only one stairway leading to the rooms on the second floor, and everyone in the lobby watched to see who went up the stairs and with whom.

When Lisa and I arrived at Caesar's, we didn't see Francisco anywhere. We assumed he was already upstairs changing clothes. A hotel employee was stationed at the foot of the stairway to ensure that only those staying at the hotel went upstairs. This was not a usual practice. Under normal circumstances, the fans, usually adults or families, were allowed to go up and talk to the bullfighters. However, because Francisco was there, several teenage girls were trying desperately to get up the stairway.

Lisa was quick to point out that she'd told me I would not be able to meet this popular young bullfighter. I pondered the situation for only a moment. Grabbing Lisa's arm, I started toward the stairway.

"Are you crazy?" Lisa gasped. "We can't go up there!"

"Just follow me," I ordered as I walked swiftly and confidently across the hotel lobby. When we reached the guard at the bottom of the stairs, I never even slowed down. I stared directly at him, giving him what I call my "I'm royalty—don't even think of touching me" look. The guard stood aside as Lisa and I proceeded up the stairway.

As we stood in the second floor hallway, Lisa looked at me and laughed. "Well, what now?"

I shook my head. "I don't know. I'll think of something."

Unfortunately, I didn't have time to make any further plans. We heard footsteps and Francisco and two other men rounded the corner. I knew I had to do something. I realized I had my program from the afternoon still in my hand. Under any other circumstances, I would die before ever asking for an autograph, but I didn't have time to think of anything else.

As soon as he finished signing, "With all my love, Francisco," I thanked him while looking directly into his deep brown eyes. He returned my gaze until I turned and walked back down the stairway. After the way we had just looked at each other, I was sure he would follow. As I reached the lobby, with Lisa right behind me, Francisco came running down the stairs.

I was able to grasp enough of his Spanish to understand that he was asking me to have dinner with him while explaining that he had to appear on a television show first. He asked if I would wait until he returned to the hotel. I told him that I might have to leave, but if I was still there when he came back I would be happy to have dinner with him. Of course, I had absolutely no intention of leaving.

When Lisa and I left later that night, Francisco walked us to my car and made me promise to come back to Tijuana when he returned in a few weeks. I promised faithfully. Little did I know that promise would change my life forever.

As promised, I did return to Tijuana. This time I had my girlfriend, Linda, with me and we had made plans to stay for the entire weekend. In our room at Caesar's, as we unpacked our suitcases, I couldn't stop talking about Francisco and the wonderful weekend we were going to have.

Saturday was a perfect day. I was able to spend a lot of time with Francisco and some other friends from Los Angeles who were also down for the weekend. Although Francisco had to retire early Saturday night, he insisted that I join the others in their rounds of the town's nightclubs.

Sunday morning Linda and I had breakfast with Francisco. He suggested that I go to the plaza to see the bulls he would face in the afternoon. I agreed and we made plans to meet when I returned to the hotel within an hour or so.

I did go to the plaza, but I did not return to the hotel. That afternoon my life nearly ended on the mountain road between Tijuana and the sea.

CHAPTER FOURTEEN

My Journey

*My spirit is going very soon to see the Great
Spirit Chief.*

—Tu-eka-kas, Nez Perce, father of Chief Joseph,
at the hour of his death, 1871

*S*everal doctors stood around me as I lay on an operating
table, barely conscious. One of them spoke in a kind voice,
assuring me that everything would be all right as they began
to prepare me for surgery. I knew that my head injuries were
very serious and I kept thinking of my young son. I didn't
want to leave him—I was his sole support and security in life.

Before I could think further, I began to lose consciousness. I remember vaguely wondering if they had given me
any anesthetic. I was still in such horrible pain that I'm sure
I wouldn't have felt the injection. Then everything went
black.

I have no idea how much time passed, but the next thing
I knew I was standing on a dirt road. To my great relief, the
pain was gone. In front of me was a hill covered with green
trees. Although I had never seen this place before, it some-

how was very familiar, as if this was not the first time I had been there. A wonderful sense of peace seemed to emanate from the shady woods.

Standing among the trees were many Native Americans. All of them were Choctaw. These were my people—all of my relatives who had lived before me; I knew I was being met by family and friends. There were also many animals waiting quietly on the hill. I knew that because we are related to all things in the universe, these were also my relations.

In the foreground was a man who stood out from all the rest. It was clear that he possessed the wisdom of all ages. The love and kindness that came forth from this man had no measure. I knew I was standing before my Creator.

I was looking at people who loved me very much, but Creator's love was by far the strongest. I felt like I was attending a wonderful family reunion. There was nothing to fear. I was looking into a world that was not strange, eerie, or unnatural. It was a wondrous place filled with love, happiness, and understanding.

Since I love animals, it was a great joy to see so many in the Spirit World. When I was a small child, I had once been taken to a Sunday school class where the teacher had remarked that there was no room in heaven for animals. I had not believed her, but it was still nice to witness the truth firsthand. I now knew for certain that we will one day be reunited with the people that we have loved and the animals that we have shared our lives with.

The strongest thing I felt while standing on that dirt road was God's absolute love. I knew this great love was not for me alone, that God's love extends to every person and every creature, that it is all encompassing.

Life and death are one. When we die, we are merely transcending into another part of our existing world. Death should not be feared because the Spirit World is filled with happiness and love.

When our body dies we are released from earthly suffering. Our spirits are free to soar above all dissention, pain, and sorrow. We truly feel the joy of God's eternal love.

When loved ones pass on into the Spirit World, it is only natural to grieve. A certain amount of grief is healthy and necessary, but do not let grief overtake your life. Those you love are still with you, as are relatives you have never known—relatives who passed into the spirit realm long before you were born.

Those who have loved you while on Earth continue to love you when they enter the Spirit World. Their love constantly surrounds you, giving you guidance and protection. They truly understand your innermost feelings. Your happiness makes them happy. If they see you grieving, they feel sadness. When on Earth, they brought joy to your life. Honor their memory by bringing joy to the lives of others.

Time on Earth is fleeting and when it passes you will join those who have gone before you. Only when your body returns to the dust of the Earth will you truly be able to move freely. Many people try to give comfort by speaking of things they believe. I not only *believe*, but I have *actually seen* the Spirit World. I *know* that when we die, we will be met by all of our relations who have lived before us.

In recent years, I have heard people arrogantly say, "I have a *personal* relationship with God," insinuating that others do not. Arrogance has no place in religion. No one person has all the answers. When we believe we know everything, we really know nothing at all. Don't make the mistake of believing that you are closer to God than anyone else. God does not love one of us more than another; His relationship with each of us is truly personal.

We have the ability, through prayer or meditation, to communicate with God at any time we wish, whether at home, on the freeway, or in church. The place of prayer does not determine the sincerity.

While attending church can be emotionally and spiritually uplifting, it will not guarantee your immediate acceptance into the Spirit World. Prayer alone will not get you there. Far more important is the way you live your life. The old saying "Actions speak louder than words" is an absolute truth.

As I stood on the road before the Spirit World, many thoughts were conveyed to me, although no words were spoken. The spoken language is only necessary for humans to communicate with each other.

I clearly understood that if I wished to do so, I could cross over into the Spirit World. I would be welcomed with an outpouring of heartfelt love and would never again feel pain. Every moment of eternity would be joyous. Yet I knew if I chose to step over into that world of peace and joy, I would never be able to return to Earth. Knowing the incredible physical pain I had just escaped from, the thought of living in the Spirit World seemed wonderful. The pain I had known had been so great, I truly did not wish to go back.

Not really wanting to look away from the Spirit World, I forced myself to look back to the other side of the road. At the edge of the road stood Jim, the young man who had once shared my life. Although we no longer lived together and did not see each other frequently, we had remained close. In Jim's arms was my son, Pete. Both of them were looking at me and it was obvious that they loved me. I knew that they wanted me to return, but I also knew they would understand if I chose not to.

When I saw my son, my choice was immediately made. So deep was my love for him that the thought of physical pain, no matter how great, was not enough to keep me away. I wanted to return to Earth.

As I looked past Jim and my son, I saw a land of total destruction. It looked like a desert, possibly after nuclear warfare. The earth was arid and barren, and the parched soil was split and cracked. The heat was incredible and I could see that the land was filled with pain. I knew that I was looking at the future of Earth, and what it would be like if man did not stop destroying God's creation.

I began to panic. I did not want my grandchildren, great-grandchildren, or future generations to experience what I was now seeing. There were no people in the scene displayed before me. When I saw that desolate land, I knew the people who had once lived there had suffered tremendously before they died.

Looking at this horrific scene, I understood that this holocaust was not a punishment from God for man's evil deeds. This destruction was man-made. Man had destroyed the Earth with selfishness, greed, and no thought or concern for future generations. Gone were the rainforests, jungles, and tropical islands. Gone were the mountains, lush valleys, and deserts covered with blooming cacti. Gone were all the animals, birds, fish, and the small crawlers of the soil. Gone were all the things that God had created. Man, the greatest enemy of nature, had done this. I felt an overwhelming sense of sadness.

I made a vow that, if I was allowed to return to Earth to care for my son, I would do everything within my power to educate people about the total destruction we are facing. Just as we humans have the ability to commit this destruction, we also have the power to reverse it.

Suddenly, I found myself looking down at doctors surrounding a woman on an operating table. I saw that I was the woman on the table and I could hear the doctors talking as they continued to operate on me. Then everything went black.

When I again heard doctors' voices, I knew I was still alive. I kept drifting in and out of consciousness as I tried to recall what had happened. I knew that I had died and traveled to the Spirit World. As weak as I was, I had a new feeling of both peace and power. No one could take my life from me. I knew that when my earthly life ended, my spiritual life would continue.

I thought about what I left behind when I chose to return to Earth. I recalled the peace and joy of the Spirit World and I remembered the overpowering love that Creator and all my relations held for me. As I lay on that operating table still undergoing surgery, I knew that my spirit relatives were with me, that their love still surrounded me. I had always believed that I was watched over and protected by Creator and also by those I had loved who were now in the Spirit World. I now knew that many more loving protectors were always with me. All of my relations who had ever lived before me truly loved me and wanted me to have the joy of living a good and meaningful life.

I understood that if I lived through this surgery and was able to recover from all of my injuries, I would have a lifetime of work ahead of me. I would have to make others realize what we are doing to ourselves and the Earth. I knew I would have to be very careful and speak strictly in a political manner. If, in 1969, I began to speak publicly about dying and returning from the dead, I would probably be hauled away in a straitjacket.

Every person is a spiritual being. Each of us has a multitude of spirit protectors who are with us at all times waiting to help us on life's journey. If we sincerely pray and leave our hearts open, we will receive our life's instructions. The instructions that Creator gives to us will benefit not only ourselves but all of mankind. These instructions will not come as voices booming out of the heavens or the hand of God writing messages on our bedroom wall. The thoughts will quietly come into our minds and we will know them to be true. Sometimes we will receive a small idea that will grow over time; other times it might be an instant powerful thought. It may be so obvious that we wonder why we hadn't thought of it earlier.

Any spiritual thoughts you receive will be productive. They will never be harmful or meanspirited. If you experience negative feelings, they are only creations of your own mind. Today murderers try to excuse their actions by saying that God or a devil told them to kill someone. Or, worse yet, they will try to explain that when they committed murder it was beyond their control because they ate Twinkies for lunch. We, as adults, are each totally responsible for our actions. We cannot blame others for our misdeeds.

The things that we must do in life—the rules that we must live by—are with us from the day we are born. We know right from wrong. Unfortunately, as we grow, learn a language, and begin to fit into the already corrupt world around us, these Original Instructions slip back into our subconscious. We must pray for a renewal of the love that was given to us at birth. Pray to find the best way to carry out God's work.

When I returned from the Spirit World, the Original Instructions I had been given at birth were once again released. Some knowledge was immediate; other truths would continue to be revealed to me over a period of years.

Time is very different in the Spirit World. I was only gone from Earth for five minutes, but I brought back knowledge and understanding that would normally take years to learn. I thought about the denial of evolution by many Christians. Because of the vast time difference between Earth and the Spirit World, the creation of man by God and the acceptance of the theory of evolution do not have to be contradictory.

The Bible tells us that God created the world and all upon it in five days. The sixth day He placed man upon the Earth and on the seventh day He rested. Seven days in the time frame of the Spirit World may be equivalent to seven million, seven hundred million, or seven billion years here on Earth. Today we know that the Earth was here more than five days before man was upon it. It was here millions and millions of years before man. That does not mean that, in God's time frame, it was not five days.

Native American nations have different, though similar, creation histories. Traditional African tribal people have their beliefs. Aboriginal Australians have beliefs unique to them. Christians have their own beliefs about creation, and Buddhists have their beliefs. All religions have different teachings, yet most believe that we were originally put on Earth by a Supreme Being.

Most of us who believe in God believe that He created all things including Earth and all that is upon it. It is true that God created man in His image. However, God's image is spiritual, not physical. Whether He created humans as we are today or God placed a speck of matter in the primeval ocean that eventually became man is not important. Whichever way it happened, God created us.

It is unfortunate that those who confess to believe in God spend so much time arguing over which religion is better. They would be much closer to God and the Spirit World if they spent that time helping others and working to heal the Earth.

We are now living in the last days we have to reverse the enormous amount of damage we have done to our sacred Mother Earth. If we continue to dump tons of trash into the ground, destroy the air and sea, create radioactive waste, and decimate our rainforests, which are the lungs of the planet, all life on Earth will end.

We can change this disastrous course, but the change must start within ourselves. When we are truly in touch with our spirituality, wars will end, pollution will cease, and we will all live together in the peaceful world that God gave to us in the beginning.

In 1994, a white buffalo calf was born in southern Wisconsin. Native Americans look upon this as a sign from Creator. This is a warning to all people who do not live in a spiritual manner—a warning that tells us that time is fast running out and that we must return to traditional thought.

Returning to traditional thought does not mean that you have to go out and live off the land. You can live in a penthouse in New York City, and if you conduct your life in a spiritual manner, you will be closer to Creator than the woodsman who lives in a little cabin and beats his wife and children.

Although I have spoken to thousands of people since my accident, until now, only those closest to me knew about my journey to the Spirit World. One of the first persons I shared my experience with was Mad Bear, a Tuscarora medicine man, who was held in great respect by Native Americans.

In 1971, Mad Bear was in Los Angeles. He and I, along with others, had flown to Sacramento to attend a political event. When we returned to Los Angeles, I had the privilege of driving Mad Bear to his various speaking engagements. This was a rare opportunity to be able to learn many things. I probably asked too many questions, but I was eager to learn as much as I could in the short time that we had together.

Mad Bear's main concern was the irresponsible and disrespectful manner in which most humans are treating the Earth. As we drove past the hills surrounding Griffith Park, a very old and large park in Los Angeles, he noticed that the tops of many of the tallest trees were leaning over, bending down toward the Earth. He explained that they were simply too sad to continue to live in this world that man is fast destroying. They were asking Mother Earth to take them back.

When I revealed that I had died on an operating table and traveled to the Spirit World, Mad Bear understood completely. We discussed at length the things I had learned. We talked about Creator and his relationship with every individual.

Mad Bear said that each person of every race is placed here by Creator and has equal importance on Earth. He expressed his strong belief in the ability of all people to bring meaningful change into their lives.

I told him what I had learned about our loss of values regarding marriage and children, about the need to protect animals and the Earth, and what must be done in order for human life to continue. Mad Bear spoke of ancient teachings that coincided with what I had learned. He said I had an important message that needed to be told. He suggested I travel around the country, speak to many different groups of people, and share the knowledge I brought back from the Spirit World.

Unfortunately, at that time, travel was an impossibility. I had to remain in one city and work to provide a home for my son, Pete, who was still in school. However, I did promise to share my teachings with as many people as possible.

My time spent in the Spirit World is as clear today as it was when I was actually there. While the wooded hill upon which Creator and all my relations stood looked familiar to me, I knew that I had never seen it before. When I was attending UCLA, I was working on a paper in the research library, looking through a book on the history of the Choctaw Nation. When I turned one page, I stopped, and my heart began pounding wildly. I was looking at a black and white photograph. The photograph was of a wooded hillside. It was the exact place that I had been when I visited the Spirit World. I read the caption below the picture. The hill was Nanih Waya, our traditional burial mound in the state of Mississippi. It is now covered with trees and resembles a rather large hill. Nanih Waya is the sacred center of our Choctaw culture.

Whenever I am faced with a challenge or confronted by an adversary, I think of Nanih Waya. It is the memory of my time in the Spirit World that I draw upon for strength. Nanih

Waya also now holds great personal meaning for me, for my beloved younger brother, Mike, who was of traditional mind and thought, is now buried there.

Sitting in the college library, looking at the picture, I felt a renewal of my own personal power. I knew where I came from and I knew where I was going. I could feel the strength of all my relations protecting me, guiding my path. I knew who I was born to be—I am a Choctaw woman.

CHAPTER FIFTEEN

One God

*Our religion is the traditions of our
ancestors—the dreams of our old men, given
them in solemn hours of night by the Great
Spirit; and the visions of our chiefs; and it is
written in the hearts of our people.*

—Seathl, Dwamish chief, 1854

There is one God—one Creator of all things. He is called
by many names, but a name is not important. As Shake-
speare said, "What's in a name? That which we call a rose by
any other name would smell as sweet."

Many Native Americans refer to God as Creator or
Grandfather. I think we use the term "grandfather" because
we know that Creator is a kind and gentle being who loves
us very much. As children, we are disciplined by our parents.
Sometimes, our grandparents are whom we gain so much
pleasure from and who often tend to spoil us. Among Native
Americans, "grandfather" is also a term of respect, given to

older men of great wisdom. They do not necessarily have to
be a blood relation.

In this book, I usually refer to Creator as God because
this is the term most frequently used by people today. But
whether I refer to the Supreme Being as God or Creator, all
terms mean the same.

God gave Original Instructions to all races and cultures
of man and showed them how to best respect, care for, and
protect the Earth in their region. These instructions may
have been brought to us by the appearance of a spiritual
being or they may have been given to prophets. They may
have been sent into the minds of our wise men and
women—our elders to whom we turn for guidance. In whatever manner God appears to us, whether as a man, as a
woman, or as simply a voice, it is the same God. When you
pray to God, your prayers come from your heart, not your
lips. It does not matter what name you call Him or Her.

God does not have form—form is of the Earth. God is
the Holy Spirit. God is not Caucasian, African, Asian, or
Native American. God created the races of man to live here
on Earth. God does not have gender. Humans were put on
Earth as male and female in order to procreate the species.

God is a spirit—a spirit of eternal love. He will appear to
each of us in the way that we can best understand and accept
Him. The spirit of God takes form only in your mind's eye.
He may appear to some people as a man; He may appear to
others as a woman. He will appear to animals in animal form.
God is the pure and Holy Spirit. It is only our eyes and minds
that give Him or Her form. We are a *spiritual* reflection of
God. God, as we see or imagine Him, is a physical reflection
of ourselves. God created us in His spiritual image. We
recreate God in our physical image. God is all-powerful and
all-knowing. He certainly has the wisdom to appear to each
of us in a form like our own.

Ten different people will see an auto accident and will describe it ten different ways. It is still the same accident. We each see God in our own image; it is still the same God.

When God believes the time is right, He will send great teachers to us. These teachers will be of such a form that we feel comfortable in their presence. The sight of them will not cause us fear or anxiety. Buddha was born in India. When Jesus Christ was born in Bethlehem, he was born a Jewish baby. God did not send a Norwegian into Israel nor did He send an Italian into India.

Today we are witnessing a worldwide spiritual revolution, the heart of which seems to be in the United States. Many people have recognized the dangerous course upon which most of the Earth's population is now traveling. Our cities are plagued with crime and violence; abuse of drugs and alcohol is rampant. We are so caught up in the daily problems of modern society that we have forgotten who we really are. Individualism appears to be a thing of the past as we have readily accepted our convenient new world of push buttons, glass, and steel. It is rare today to find a person who displays pride in his or her work or exhibits truly fine craftsmanship. We are quickly becoming more like functional robots rather than feeling human beings. Surrounded by modern technology in a fast-moving world, people are searching for something spiritual to guide them.

Unfortunately, people who are sincerely seeking spiritual truths are sometimes taken advantage of by false prophets. We have seen the horrors of Guyana and Waco. We have seen television evangelists fall from grace. Some pastors tell their followers to have a personal relationship with God, but it often appears that the personal relationship is with the church leader. He tells his followers how to live; he teaches politics from the pulpit; he clearly tells his congregation how much to donate to his church.

Church can provide spiritual enrichment, but you still must think for yourself. Create a *true* personal relationship with God. Let your heart listen to God's wishes. Don't put all your faith in an earthly man or woman who may be more interested in your bank account than your soul.

Many people are now traveling the United States and Europe claiming to be Native American medicine men or an apprentice to a Native American spiritual leader. It is amazing that when these so-called "apprentices" tell you the name of their spiritual leader, Native Americans have never heard of the person. We know who our spiritual leaders are. We respect and treasure them. We, as native people, feel very sorry for anyone who is misled by these charlatans. They are not what they claim to be—they are selling phony ceremonies to those eager to learn Native American ways. When Native Americans explain that these are not true ceremonies and ask them to stop, the person leading the ceremony many times will become angry or even violent. No traditional Native American would ever take money for performing a ceremony. Native American ceremonies are for Native Americans. If you are not a Native American, you will not benefit by attending these ceremonies. You can fool yourself by believing you are receiving some kind of benefit, but you cannot fool Creator. These ceremonies were given to Native Americans to be used by Native Americans. They simply will not bring power to other people. Everyone is looking for something mystical and magical. The magic is already within you. Ask God for the power to release it so that you may better work in His service.

Each person has power. Each culture has power. Each race of man has power. God had a plan when He placed every individual into a certain race and culture. When you bring spirituality into your life, you will truly take pride in the person you were born to be.

There are many ways that non-native people can work with Native Americans. We openly welcome those who come to us with sincere hearts. We will be happy to both teach you and learn from you. We can share knowledge for better understanding, but approach us with honesty as a non-native person. Please don't try to tell us your grandmother was a Cherokee princess. We must take pride in our individuality and find beauty in the way that Creator made us. We each must march to the sound of our own drum. Accept who you are and thank Creator for your life.

When people turn to another race of people for validation, they are not accepting the beauty of their own people. We are all different; in His divine wisdom, Creator made us so. We must appreciate our differences. We are equal, but we are not the same. Your race and traditions are as beautiful and as meaningful as ours. You simply need to look back far enough to find them.

Though we are different, we are all related, not just to each other, but to all things in the universe. Only when you understand your relationship, your oneness with the universe and all its powers, will your spirit find peace. The sacred spiritual core of the universe is really everywhere. It is within each of us.

We must revive our sense of shared humanity with people of all races and cultures. Positive change begins with the individual. We can *do* anything we want with ourselves and our lives, but we can only *be* what we were born to be. We all share this planet and we must share it in peace. We can learn from and support each other. We can respect each other and develop long-lasting friendships. We can live side by side on Earth and work together. But we cannot change who we are and we should not try to do so.

I meet people daily whom I call spiritual wanderers. They don't know who they really are. They may know that their parents came from Ireland, but they know nothing about the history of Ireland and its people. In America we have grown accustomed to the term "melting pot." If that is defined as a place where people can live together in peace, that is wonderful. Unfortunately, many people believe that once you are in the United States, it doesn't matter where your ancestors are buried or where your family lived before coming to America.

Native Americans believe that knowing about your ancestors makes you a whole person. In 1854, Seathl, a Dwamish chief of great stature, spoke to Isaac Stevens, Governor of the Washington Territory. He said, "To us the ashes of our ancestors are sacred and their resting place is hallowed ground. You wander far from the graves of your ancestors and seemingly without regret."

With all the problems facing Americans today, one of the biggest is lack of respect for one's self. When we learn who we are and develop self-respect, only then can we move forward and respect others.

God made different races of people and put us in different places on this Earth. God had a reason for doing this. Each race of people and each person in that race were molded by the hand of God. Each one of us is special and each one of us is important. When we say it is not important where our family originated from or we don't care anything about our past culture, we are denying a part of ourselves and a part of God's original plan for us.

Self-pride should never be boastful; rather, it should give us the confidence to lead worthwhile and meaningful lives. In a modern and technical society we seldom think of honor, yet in most traditional Native American societies, honor played a very key role. In tribal life, dishonorable actions would bring shame upon the perpetrator as well as his immediate family and kin. When we know who we are and where we came from, we feel a responsibility to act appropriately. As a creation of God and as one who is greatly loved by God, we should never act in any other manner.

We must make a strong effort to recapture our sense of morality through living a spiritual life. In the United States today, most people tend to think of themselves first. People living in a large city do not feel safe unless their homes have security systems. In Los Angeles County, people have been shot while simply driving their car on a freeway. More than 100 die every month from gunshot wounds. Beyond this are deaths by strangulation, stabbing, or other methods. When a natural disaster occurs, looting follows. After the terrible earthquake in Kobe, Japan, there was no looting. When the kidnapping of the Lindberg baby occurred, the French referred to it as "crime L'American" because there was no single word in the French language for such an act. And, of course, none of us will ever forget the horror of the April 1995 bombing of the Federal Building in Oklahoma City, where so many lives were senselessly taken. All of us realize that something must be done to bring about change in our destructive society. Change does not start from without—it starts from within. Peace does not have a chance unless it first begins in the mind of each individual.

In the midst of the confusion and turmoil of our daily lives, people are searching for inner peace and spiritual identity. Every year, people seeking truth flock to Machu Picchu in Peru, Lake Titicaca in Bolivia, or Bali trying to get in touch with their spiritual self. If you truly wish to reach the spirit within you, you don't have to go anywhere. God is always with you and ready to help if you will only ask. Don't travel without—travel within.

There is nothing wrong with visiting another person's church or religious ceremony if someone of that faith invites you to do so. You may learn something very valuable. Take that knowledge back and share it with the people of your faith. Traditional spiritual leaders of Native American nations have always listened with respect and interest to the beliefs of others. True spiritual leaders always have an open mind. This does not mean that they are going to now follow another religion. It simply means that they have listened to someone else and possibly learned something new. The greater the leader, the more he or she continues to learn.

The more we learn, the more doors will open for us. Knowledge greatly enriches our lives. In recent years I have talked to many people who are seriously trying to expand their understanding of religion. Many are looking back to the old religions that were in existence before Christianity.

Many Native Americans who are Christians are learning about their tribal religions and participating in those ceremonies. Since Christianity was first brought into Native American nations, most people still living on reservations have participated in traditional ceremonies, in addition to attending Christian church. Now, more and more Native Americans are returning to their traditional religions.

Many Christians, while still regularly attending their churches, are attempting to learn about the religion their ancestors practiced before the advent of Christianity. Some are even practicing the ancient prayers and ceremonies of the country of their origin.

To find your way back to your traditional original religion while continuing to practice a more modern religion is not a contradiction. There is but one God. When we pray, no matter what language we use or which name we call God, as long as our prayers are sincere and from the heart, God hears us.

Many of the ceremonies of the early earth religions evolved into what we now recognize as Christian holidays. The Teutonic fire festival day of the Germanic people and Winter Eve later became the Eve of All Saints' Day, which later became Halloween. April 30, the eve of St. Walpurga, was originally the eve of May Day, which for the Romans had been the fertility festival of the Floralia. In the north, this was greeted by the renewal rites associated with the maypole and the "green man." Midsummer Eve, the climax of the fire and fertility rites celebrating the triumph of the sun and renewed vegetation, became the eve of St. John the Baptist. An ancient fire festival that occurred on February 1 was transformed into the Christian Candlemas. The Christian Epiphany on January 6 coincides with the birth of the Egyptian God, Osiris. The birth date of the Persian God of the sun, Mithras, was December 25, the same date celebrated as the birth of Christ.

In traditional Native American religions, our holy men have never said, "Ours is the only religion, the true religion. If you do not believe as we do, you will go to hell." We believe man's hell is here on Earth. We each create our own living hell.

Many times, we make the mistake of trying to make rules for God. We claim we know what God looks like. We believe we know whether or not He will soon appear on Earth. We claim to know how every person on Earth should pray to God. We are like naughty children trying to make rules for a parent. Nothing is more dangerous than a person who believes he knows everything—a person who is opinionated, but uninformed.

Ninety-four percent of all Americans profess a belief in God. Many people attend church regularly, give to charities, and consider themselves spiritual beings. However, people cannot be spiritual if they think they have the power to discredit the beliefs, cultures, and religions of other people.

Never be too proud to ask God for help—God always hears your prayers. Ask for strength—strength of mind. Ask to be cleansed of any hatred within you. A spiritual person will always have an open mind and heart toward others. If you are to carry out God's work, you must learn to love and understand, not condemn.

Ask God to heal your life, open your heart to love and acceptance, and direct your thoughts. Ask God to grant you the strength to make positive changes, to free your mind from thoughts of hatred, prejudice, jealousy, and greed. As long as these thoughts occupy your mind, you will forever live in bondage, a prisoner of your own misguided thoughts. The violence in our minds contributes to the violence of our times. When your mind is filled with thoughts of hate, your heart will never know peace.

When we ask God for help, we receive strength. Prayer gives us power and opens our hearts to peace. People who are spiritually strong are able to absorb and rise above the evil that comes their way.

Your spirit is living within you, begging to be put into service. Release the power of your spirit. Allow yourself to live a full life and to be a happy person. Allow yourself to be surrounded by the divine glory of God.

Religion should be a personal relationship between you and God. God has a special life plan for each of us. When we open our hearts and minds to the will of God, we will begin to carry out this plan.

Try to find time each day for a quiet period when your mind will be open to new thoughts and ideas. There is a popular saying that a mind is like a door—it only works when it is open. If you are driving alone in your car, turn off the radio and try not to think about anything in particular. See what new thoughts come into your mind. Go into your backyard. Sit or lie under a shady tree and watch the clouds moving above you. Walk on the beach at dawn or sunset. Listen to the gulls. Listen to the sea. If you live in a large city and you can't find a blade of grass within walking distance, simply turn off your telephone, television, and radio, and sit down in a comfortable chair or lie on your bed or sofa. If you run or jog every day, do it alone and without headphones. Open your mind to receive messages and spiritual direction. Listen to the wind. Listen to the rain. At night, look toward the stars. When you dream, hold your dreams closely and search for their true meanings.

Your best spiritual thoughts will come when you are alone. In our traditional Native American nations, many young men went on vision quests. This was a time when they sought messages or signs from Creator. This was done to give better direction and meaning to their lives. They did not go on these quests in a group; they went alone. Even in our modern, frantic lives, find time each day to be alone. This is the way to communicate with Creator.

The thoughts you receive may not seem earth-shattering. One example may be something as simple as remembering a friend you haven't talked to in a long time. That may be a message for you to call that friend. Possibly that old friend has a new line of thought to share with you that could be important to your future.

Ask God to let us exchange our thoughts with His and allow us to view the world through His loving eyes. God does not look for the bad in each person; he concentrates on the good. Likewise, we must try to find the positive qualities in each individual and not dwell on the negative.

You should not *fear* God, but *love* God, trust in Him and know that He can heal all pain. When you accept God's Holy Spirit into your life, you will never have to fear, for you are truly in the hand of God.

When you free your heart of hatred, greed, prejudice, and all other evil, your mind will be clear to communicate with God. If our minds are filled with love, they will be open to receive instruction from Him and we will have the power to do God's will. Each individual represents God on Earth. We are here to carry out His wishes. We have the power to save our lives and our world.

CHAPTER SIXTEEN

Love Yourself

*I am a red man. If the Great Spirit had
desired me to be a white man he would have
made me so in the first place . . . Each man
is good in his sight. It is not necessary for
eagles to be crows.*

—Sitting Bull, Hunkpapa, 1876

One of the most important lessons, yet sometimes the hardest, is to learn to love and accept ourselves. We are God's creation and therefore are capable of great things. Every person on Earth has a purpose and each is deeply loved by God.

When the Spirit World opened before me, I was clearly shown that Creator, in His wisdom, made different races of people and put these culturally diverse peoples on different parts of our sacred Mother Earth. Each group is unique. We were created differently for a reason. If God had wanted us to be the same, He would have made us so in the beginning.

If an artist had only one color of paint, he could not paint a picture. God is the supreme artist of life. He chose different colors to create the races of man and then placed them on Earth.

Be proud of who you are. Never try to be someone you are not—to do so is to question God's judgment. God does not make mistakes. You may occasionally fool others, but you will never fool God. When you find your true place in life, your true self, you will experience the greatest peace and joy imaginable and you will truly soar with the eagles.

Each race of people was created to live on Earth in certain areas and was given Original Instructions. Our instructions may have been different, but they were right for us and for our part of the world.

As we moved into modern times, many of us wandered far from our homelands and far from our original teachings. Some of us no longer know our Original Instructions given to us by God. We need to look back and find ourselves and the teachings first given to us.

Every day we see people who are truly lost. Whenever we watch the evening news we see reports of murder, theft, and drug, alcohol, and child abuse. Each person who commits these atrocities was once an innocent child. Something happened to turn that innocence into evil. Some people will say, "The devil made them do it." This is nothing but an excuse to not take responsibility for one's actions. If you feel bad about yourself, it is easy to do bad things. A good life begins with love of self.

When we come into this world, we are pure and completely innocent. We do not know hatred or prejudice. We do not know greed. These are things we learn from life, not from God.

We are born with the ability to lead good and meaningful lives. Our feet are already on a spiritual road. In our lifetime, no matter how far we stray, if we choose to do so, we can always return to our spiritual path.

The first step on this path is to truly thank God for the life He has given you. Accept who you are and be grateful for the person God created and continues to love. Strive to be the best you can be—self-improvement shows appreciation of the gift of life.

You are a creation of God. Never allow yourself or others to see you as anything less. If you have feelings of self-hatred, get rid of them. You created the feelings. No one can hurt your feelings unless you allow them to do so. People who harbor negative feelings are always looking for an escape. Many try to find that escape with the help of drugs or alcohol or turn to the false security of becoming a gang member. Others take their anger and sense of inadequacy out on people around them through verbal or physical abuse.

Prejudice is another evil that grows out of lack of self-worth. When people have strong feelings of self-doubt, it is quite common for them to belittle others in order to feel better about themselves. In the United States, feelings of prejudice have lessened in recent years, but we still have a long way to go.

Nothing is going to make you truly happy until you are first happy with yourself. Only then can you enjoy meaningful relationships with others and the world around you. You cannot truly love another person unless you first love yourself. When you truly love yourself you will not need to cling to someone else to find happiness or to feel like a whole and complete person. You will then be able to be more selective about others in your life. You will not stay with a person who is abusive or disrespectful toward you. You will receive the respect you know you deserve. You will be free to fully love another person. This is the cornerstone of all lasting, meaningful relationships.

A problem that has developed within the past thirty years is Caucasians claiming to be Native Americans. This is usually due to a lack of pride and self-identity. It is difficult to go to a Native American function and not meet at least one

Caucasian claiming to be from one tribe or another. They will usually say that their grandmother was a Cherokee princess.

Many Native American causes are actively supported by Caucasians. Their sincere help is always welcome. However, quite often within a short period of time, they are dying their hair black, wearing instant tanning lotion, and claiming to be Native Americans. How tragic that they cannot find pride in their own race. In traditional tribal cultures both honesty and pride in self-identity were held in high regard. When a person pretends to be someone he or she is not, that person is acting in a manner totally opposite to true Native American beliefs.

I am a Choctaw woman. If I chose to do so, I could convince myself that I am really Danish. The only person I would fool would be myself. No matter how much I would want to change, I could never be Danish. Others would not think I was Danish; they would only think I was crazy.

"Pan-Indianism" is a term that is being used more frequently. I believe the phrase was originally coined to describe the unity of all Native American nations. However, today, many people mistakenly believe that Pan-Indianism means that all Native Americans are the same and that we all share the same traditions.

While it is true that in recent years Native Americans have made strong attempts to work together, we will always remain separate nations with our own cultures and beliefs (just as Germany and Italy are different countries with their own cultures and holidays within the continent of Europe).

Sadly, some Native Americans will travel far to participate in ceremonies of other Native American nations. This is not because they have married into that nation or because a *true* spiritual leader has asked them to participate. It is because they have not learned their own ceremonies. This is yet another example of people not taking pride in who they really are. Native Americans who know their own heritage are very proud of their individual nations.

The way we view ourselves determines how we act. If we don't believe in ourselves, no one else will either. Tap into the spiritual power within you. Know how strong and perfect you are. Be yourself. You, on Earth, are a reflection of the Creator.

In traditional Native American culture, one's tribe or nation is very important. Knowing who we are gives us our balance and allows us to walk in harmony upon the Earth. When we look at the world today, it is apparent that something is drastically wrong. Many of our problems begin with our lack of pride and self-identity.

God has a plan for each of us. You may be given direction through dreams. A message may suddenly come to you as you are walking. An entirely new positive plan may be conceived while you are driving your car. When your mind is open, it is amazing what you can learn. Do everything possible to open your mind and heart to receive instruction from God.

Begin to research your history by talking to everyone in your family as well as people who knew members of your family who are now deceased. Remember, you are only trying to find out the country of origin of your family.

Family surnames rarely existed before 1300 in western countries. A person was known as Edward the baker, Edward the butcher, Edward the blacksmith, Edward of the hill, Edward by the stream, etc. Due to the increase in population, "of" and "the" were eventually dropped and surnames came into being. So if your last name is Hill, probably 600 or 700 years ago one of your relatives lived somewhere on a hill.

"Son" or "sen" at the end of a word means that at one time it was "son of." The name Emson used to be "son of Emma" and Pearson was "son of Piers or Peter."

If you are of European descent, carefully check the accuracy of both first and last names. Many times names were changed when immigrants entered the United States.

If you need help in locating your country of origin, write to the Church of Jesus Christ of Latter-day Saints (LDS), also known as the Mormon Church. You do not have to be a church member and they have extensive archives you can access for your search. Write to Family History Library, 35 North West Temple Street, Salt Lake City, Utah 84150, or visit the LDS branch library closest to where you live.

This search for self-discovery will not only be rewarding but also very enjoyable. There is nothing to fear. This is a search for your true self, not an exposé of long-forgotten relatives. You want to know where your ancestors came from, not if your grandfather was a horse thief or your grandmother sang in saloons.

The search for your heritage does not have to be difficult. You do not have to know what village your people lived in or what their occupations were. You simply want to know which country your ancestors came from. Today in the United States, most people are a mixture of several nationalities. When doing your research, try to determine which nationality in your background is predominant. Trace back to the earliest times possible. What was the religion then? What ceremonies did the people hold? Were the majority of the people farmers, hunters, sailors, or craftsmen? What role did women play in society? Learn as much as you can. Once you have found your ancestral roots, proudly accept who you are. By fully accepting yourself as God created you, you will open your mind to new thought. It is now possible to move forward and learn to love yourself.

To truly love yourself, you must also forgive yourself. All of us are human. All of us have made mistakes. You may not be proud of the life you are now living; however, you do have a choice. Anytime you wish, you can change your behavior and your life. Acknowledge that the past belongs to yesterday. Ask God to forgive you—then forgive yourself. Accept God's forgiveness. Learn from your mistakes, but don't let guilt poison your life. Put the past behind you and start over.

We are all spiritual beings—the power of God is within each of us. We must learn to release that power. All people have the potential to carry out God's work and we must fulfill that potential. When we live each day to the best of our ability, our feet will be firmly planted on the spiritual path. There is no reason to turn back. We must never listen to others who cruelly try to hurt or humiliate us. We must be confident in the goodness of our own actions. Above all, we must remember that we are a creation of God's divine love.

CHAPTER SEVENTEEN

The Natural Order

*We sang songs that carried in their melodies
all the sounds of nature—the running of
waters, the sighing of winds, and the call of
the animals. Teach these to your children
that they may come to love nature
as we love it.*

—Grand Council Fire of American Indians, 1927

*A*ll things in the universe are related. Creator placed all creatures on Earth to live in balance and harmony. Every bird in the sky, every insect that crawls, and every blade of grass are important in His sight. We should never believe that we are superior to any other creature; we are simply different. Only God has dominion over the Earth. When man claims to have dominion over other creatures, his statement is political, not spiritual.

In the Old Testament of the Bible, in Ecclesiastes, Chapter 3, Verses 19 and 20, it says:

For that which befalleth the sons of men befalleth beasts; even one thing befalleth them: as the one dieth, so dieth the other; yea, they have all one breath; so that a man hath no preeminence above a beast: for all is vanity.

All go unto one place; all are of the dust, and all turn to dust again.

There was a time in all cultures when the Earth and everything upon it was respected. Unfortunately, as populations grew so did greed. The result has been disastrous. Today our world is completely out of balance.

From the tiny creatures that crawl in the soil to the winged creatures of the air, all are equally loved by God. Ghandi said, "The greatness of a nation . . . can be judged by the way its animals are treated."

Our relationship with other creatures inhabiting the Earth can be very strong and it does not end after death. Animals pass over into the Spirit World and are welcomed by God the same way as humans are. People who truly love animals can take comfort in knowing that, one day, they will once again be reunited with their pets who have gone on before them.

When my beloved poodle, Chum Boy, died, I was out of the state. I returned home the next day and my son broke the tragic news to me. I was absolutely overcome by grief. Later that evening, when I was sitting in bed, fully awake and with a bright light on, I heard familiar scampering footsteps in the hallway outside of my bedroom. Somehow, I was not surprised to see Chum Boy run into the room and jump up on my bed and into my arms. I held him for only a second before he ran from the room. In the next moment, I once again heard his little feet racing across the floor. He scurried into my bedroom and up into my arms once more. I held him tightly until he jumped down and ran out of the door.

I knew that in my lifetime on Earth I would not be able to hold him again, although I would think of him every day and dream of him often.

As I reflected on what had just occurred, I realized that Chum Boy had looked different than the last time I had seen him. I realized that his body had been that of a younger dog's and his hair had been dark black, instead of the grayish-black of his later years. He was young and healthy again.

I knew that because I had not been there when he died, he had to come back to say good-bye. Chum Boy always had to have his own way about everything. I'm sure that's why he came back not only once but twice. Chum Boy always did whatever he wanted, whenever he wanted. Creator certainly has His hands full in the Spirit World with that little one.

When an animal's life is taken, it must be done with respect, and only when food is needed. No part of it should be wasted; otherwise, it should not be killed. In our lives, we eat the flesh of our animal brothers and sisters. When we die, the small creatures of the soil eat our flesh. They in turn feed the larger creatures. This completes the sacred circle of life.

Species of animals are disappearing from the Earth at an alarming rate. When man destroys a species, either by intent or by encroaching upon its territory, he is destroying a creation of God. This is a creature that God put upon the Earth and He intended for that species to remain on Earth.

To live our lives in a sacred manner, we must respect all life. God created each thing upon the Earth and every thing has a spirit. We, as humans, are not the wisest of creatures. We may have the most technical knowledge, but we are not the wisest. Unfortunately, we are the most destructive.

In the overall passage of time, man is only one small second in the hour that there has been life on Earth. Yet, in that one short second, he has almost destroyed the Earth. In the last fifty years mankind has come close to the point of no return.

When we overpopulate, we destroy our environment. When old European cities were overcrowded, plagues greatly diminished the populace. Creator continuously warns us against overpopulation, but most people refuse to listen. In recent years the warnings have become intense. We have experienced many deadly earthquakes, and there have been floods in areas that have not been flooded in years. People have lost their homes to hurricanes and tidal waves. Volcanoes that have been dormant for centuries are now erupting. These are warnings to stop the destruction and turn back to our Original Instructions. The Earth will not take much more. If we do not change our way of living and find harmony with nature, life on Earth as we know it will end. This is not speculation—it is a scientific fact.

When I see the terrible damage being done to the Earth today, I am able to understand the nightmares of my childhood. I was being shown what would happen if modern man and his destructive methods, such as strip mining, nuclear waste, and the destruction of all natural habitats, keep marching forward. If man refuses to see or listen to the cries of the Earth, there will be no way for any of us to avoid the total impending disaster.

We have in our power the ability to stop the two most destructive actions against the Earth today. The first and the greatest danger to all of us is overpopulation. The Earth's population is presently increasing by 90 million a year. Tribal people understand the fine balance between human life and the Earth. To overpopulate a region is to destroy it. There are many millions of acres on Earth where no humans live. This does not mean, however, that the Earth can support a larger number of people. The Earth can only provide a certain amount of water and food. Animals seem to understand this a lot better than humans. Wolves bond with a lifetime mate. Only the pack leader's mate will bear young.

If it is a year of little food, even they do not breed. We could certainly take a lesson from the wolves.

The second greatest threat, which is destroying the Earth and all life upon it, is the pollution caused by overpopulation. To pollute is a direct action against God for we are harming the world that He has created.

Rainforests are the lungs of the Earth. Half the medicine known to man comes from these forests, yet every minute 75 more acres of rainforest are destroyed forever. That is more than 39 million acres per year. The bare land is only productive for a few years and then will become barren waste, where before there was a lush forest and half the medicine known to man. Man is destroying the rainforests.

In only ten minutes, a logger with a chain saw can cut down a tree that took one thousand years to grow and has a thirty-three-foot-wide trunk. Eighty percent of all the Earth's surface vegetation is found in the rainforests. *Fifty percent of all the oxygen we breathe comes from the rainforests.* Man is destroying the rainforests.

It is hard to find a person who does not know someone who has died from cancer. We all pray for a cure. Each and every day around the world, one hundred species of plant life disappear. Only one percent of rainforest plants has been assessed for their medicinal value. An estimated four million forms of plant and animal life exist in rainforests. Man is destroying the rainforests.

We must stop destroying the Earth. If you believe that God created the Earth, you will not destroy that which God created. Start by making a list of things you can do to stop this horrible path of destruction.

You can begin by recycling. Recycle everything. Look on the bottom of plastic containers for a number in a triangle. Don't forget shampoo bottles, dish soap bottles, etc.—anything that is plastic. Most recycling centers will take plastic with numbers one and two. It is a little harder to find a place to take the containers with the higher numbers. Always recycle glass and metal. If you buy cardboard cans of frozen juice, take a bottle opener and pry the metal lids off each end of the cardboard so that the metal can be recycled. It takes a glass bottle one million years to decompose back into the Earth. Please, stop and seriously think about what we are doing to this Earth that God has created. Every time you do not recycle, it is a direct act against God.

Those in touch with the Earth understand that the land can take no more. Pollution has thrown all life completely out of balance. Before man began his destruction of land, sea, and air, life on Earth moved in continuous harmony.

Traditional Native American belief tells us that the Earth does not belong to us. We belong to the Earth. We have a sacred duty to protect it and in our every act return thanks for the gift of life.

Above human rights there are natural rights—protection of all creatures, Earth, and the universe. Only when we learn to respect ourselves and treat ourselves as sacred will we respect all things and know that all things are sacred. When we live with respect for natural rights, our lives will greatly improve and our minds will be able to receive, accept, and understand the knowledge given to us by God.

CHAPTER EIGHTEEN

Marriage and Children

These tribes here all spoke with one word in saying that they look after their children for seven generations to come, and I think it is right.

—Dead Eyes, Sioux, 1875

*M*arriage is the cornerstone of any nation; it provides the environment that raises the leaders of tomorrow. A nation is only as strong as its children, for those children are the future leaders. They are the ones who will have the responsibility of protecting the Earth. They will care for their parents in their elder years. That is why all religions place such a high value upon children. Children hold a special place in the sacred circle of life. The lack of family bonds and values is the beginning of most of mankind's problems today.

A happy marriage is the basis for a strong family structure. Many of the problems we currently face—drug use, alcoholism, spousal and child abuse, gangs, and violent crime—can often be traced back to an unhappy childhood without the benefit of two loving parents.

Unfortunately, in the United States today people seem to view marriage very casually. The divorce rate is incredibly high and more and more people choose to live together without marriage. I believe this is, at least partly, due to observing so many others who are unhappily married.

I realize that in my teenage years I made many mistakes. I should have insisted that Pete and I get married before I consented to have his baby. I'm sure it would have been much better for our child. My son, Pete, along with my second son, Na Humma, have given me the greatest joy in my life, but I know Pete's life would have been easier if his father and I had been a happily married couple. I, of course, believed that we would one day marry, but I was not yet experienced enough to understand the harsh realities of life. I still believed in the knight in shining armor carrying me off on his fast steed, but Pete was not that knight and he rode around in a pickup truck, not on a horse.

Marriage should be a union of two souls. A strong marriage will have equal partners. Neither partner should be dominant—there must be give and take on both sides. A person should stay in a marriage because the marriage provides love and happiness, not because of legal or financial constraints.

A strong marriage will continue to grow and constantly renew itself. The success of that renewal depends on the daily choices made by both you and your partner. Never view your partner's needs as less important than your own. In all of your choices, before you commit any act, consider the effect it will have upon your marriage.

Trust is necessary for a good marriage. You cannot truly love someone you cannot trust. When you married, you took vows and those vows must be kept. If you trust your spouse, you will allow your spouse freedom. Know that wherever he or she is, the vows you made when you married will never be forgotten or broken. Though you may sometimes be apart, your hearts will always be as one.

Do not feel jealousy over any past relationships of your spouse. If your spouse still has feelings for a person in his or her past, that is not a bad thing. Ending a relationship does not necessarily mean an end to caring. To continue to care about the welfare and happiness of someone in the past should not be viewed as a threat to a new relationship. To have such feelings simply shows that your partner is a loving, caring person. If your spouse is sticking pins into a replica of an old flame or using his or her picture for target practice, then you really do have reason to worry.

Our modern day lifestyles have become so busy that we tend to overlook the things that are really important. Each day, set aside time to talk to each other. More importantly, take the time to listen. When your partner speaks, listen with complete attention. Let your partner know that you believe his or her words are important. Find joy, not jealousy, in your spouse's success. Show compassion for any failures. Do not be afraid to express and demonstrate your love for one another everyday. Understand the importance of patience. Be strong enough to be gentle. Before you undertake any action, ask yourself if you are setting a good example for your children. When you find yourself angry, stop and re-member all of your spouse's good qualities before you speak.

If you feel anger, discuss your feelings with your partner. Explain what triggers these feelings. Suppressed anger will only grow stronger. If you disagree with your partner, discuss the subject thoroughly. It is important to allow your partner to get angry and verbally express that anger, but make a firm commitment to never go to sleep without forgiving your partner for anything that made you angry.

It is a rare relationship where the partners do not expe-rience occasional anger. However, there is no reason for a man or woman to ever raise a hand against, or even push or shove, the other. This is totally and completely unacceptable in a marriage or any other situation. Children who witness violence in their own home will many times repeat this violence when they are adults. It is hard to imagine a peaceful, safe country if the homes within that country are not safe and peaceful also.

Let your marriage be a shelter, a cushion, and a buffer against life's problems—a safe harbor from the storm. A good marriage will give you strength. Marriage provides a foundation so that together you can carry out God's intended work. Let your home be a joyful place that you look forward to returning to at the end of the day. Laugh together, love together, and share together, and your life will be filled with joy.

When the spirit of God is in a relationship, you will not judge or look for fault in your partner. You will not speak out in anger, but offer support, forgiveness, and understanding. You will focus on the strength, goodness, and joy in your relationship rather than seek out the weaknesses.

Whatever material things you gain or lose, if there is strength in your marriage, you will survive any loss of possessions. When people live through natural disasters, their first response is usually, "I lost my house, but thank God my family is all right. Nothing else really matters."

The truly important things in life cannot be taken from you. When you lose a loved one, it is only a temporary loss. You will be together again in the Spirit World. You may lose worldly possessions, but the really valuable things—love, courage, kindness, gentleness, compassion, understanding, generosity, joy, inner peace, faith, hope, and the belief in God—can never be taken away.

Children do not belong to their parents. They belong to all people and to the world. They are to be loved and respected, but they are not possessions. They are individuals who share in the life of the family. No two children are alike and therefore should not be treated in the same manner. Children have unique thoughts and rights. You as a parent are not a warden in a jail, but rather a nurturer of young life. Do not break their spirits with excessive discipline. Give your children the freedom to make mistakes, but always protect them from danger. To hit a child simply expresses to the child that you have neither the intelligence nor the control to find a verbal solution, and your actions show them that problems can only be settled by violence. It also demonstrates a bullying tactic where it is all right for a strong, large person to strike a weaker, smaller one. Your child will learn by watching you.

Children must be listened to and their thoughts and ideas treated with respect and deep consideration. A child learns by example. A child will learn patience if he or she is shown patience. Children must know that even though you may sometimes not agree with their actions, they will always have your unconditional love.

Life goes forward. Do not try to turn your children into carbon copies of yourself. You gave them life, but God gave them their spirit. Give them the freedom to make their own choices.

An African proverb wisely states "It takes a whole village to raise a child." Today, however, more than half of the children in the United States will spend a significant part of their childhoods without a father in the home. Thirty percent of all children are born to unmarried women. The United States has the highest rate of teen pregnancy in the industrialized world. Many, many children grow up today totally lacking in the ideals and values that a father could provide. It is a very sad fact that people are beginning to view a fatherless home as normal.

I feel especially blessed that my son, Pete, has grown into such an exceptionally fine young man. Considering that I was a teenage mother and that he was raised in a rather unconventional, single-parent household, he could have turned out much differently. Even though I did the best I could, I still wish I could have provided him with a stable, two-parent home.

Teach your children the value of all life. Teach them respect for humans, animals, plants, and all things upon Earth. But as you teach your children, also take time to learn from them. Their thoughts are new and represent the future.

In traditional societies, respect for elders is a very important part of everyday life. Teach your children to respect their elders for they carry the traditions and wisdom of your ancestors. From the time that your children are very young, encourage them to learn their family's history. When you have family gatherings, set aside a time for the children to sit quietly and listen to their elders.

Respect for the elderly is an accepted value among tribal people. It is even practiced in some groups of animals. If an elephant whose herds are governed by females sees one of its young being disrespectful to an elder, the mother will strongly discipline her calf.

When your children are older, involve them in environmental or charity projects or volunteer work. Make this a fun experience. Listen to and be grateful for their input and suggestions. Let them understand the importance of helping others and working to protect and heal our sacred Mother Earth. They must understand that our future is in their hands. They have the power to change tomorrow.

If your family has very limited financial resources and survival has been a struggle, express to your children the importance of education to change their difficult lifestyle. If your family is financially secure, instill in your children the belief that the more you have, the more important it is to give back. They must learn gratitude for all of life's gifts.

With most species, protection of the young is a natural instinct. With musk oxen, the entire herd will encircle the young and fight to the death to protect them. When baby gorillas are taken from the wild by poachers to be sold to zoos or circuses, it is usually necessary to kill several adults in the group because they will attack poachers in order to save one of their young.

In many countries today, the welfare of children is still a priority. Unfortunately, in the United States, every year more and more benefits are denied to our children. School budgets are continuously cut and children as young as seven years old are found with guns at school. A country that depends on uneducated children to direct its future will not survive in today's world.

Children used to be the pride and joy of their parents. Families were strong and pulled together as a unit. In recent times, the priority seems to have moved from children to material possessions. These priorities are also reflected in the business world. Factories continuously pollute the Earth without considering the damage to future generations. Children are our tomorrow. They are our hope to bring peace and light to a deeply troubled world.

A traditional Native American belief is that before you act, look ahead and see how that action will affect the seventh generation. If your intended action will not have positive results for the children seven generations in the future, choose another action. You accepted life's greatest responsibility when you chose to bring a child into this world. Your children must always come first.

CHAPTER NINETEEN

The Welfare of the People

You shall look and listen to the welfare of the whole people, and have always in view, not only the present but the coming generations—the unborn of the future nation.

—Constitution of the Iroquois Federation,
1400s or earlier

Each day we live is a gift from God and we should give thanks daily for the gift of life. We must express our thanks by giving back to creation. I not only begin and end each day with prayer, I pray many, many times each day. When I pray, I may ask for strength or guidance. I may give thanks for something that just occurred. I silently talk to God. I do not pray out loud to try to make others notice me. My relationship with Creator is truly personal.

Many people today claim to be spiritual but fail to live in a spiritual manner. This leads to the downfall of our societies and the destruction of the Earth. I personally know people who study their religion constantly, attend religious meetings, never miss church, and send checks to charities. I have never seen them ladling soup in a skid row shelter, starting recycling drives in their neighborhoods, picking up trash along the seashore, or doing anything to really help other people or heal the Earth.

The ability to aggravate or heal the Earth's problems is within every individual. We each have the power to make these changes. Being in touch with our own spiritual power enables us to help others and the Earth. It also brings greater strength, happiness, and a sense of well-being into our own lives.

When we do not have love in our lives, we experience a feeling of emptiness. Some people spend a lifetime looking for love. The absence of love is sometimes misinterpreted as a need for a lover. Love must begin within ourselves. We must express our love through acts of kindness toward others. Kindness and compassion are our greatest virtues. Our acts of love are carried out through sharing, helping, accepting, and never judging others.

Only by allowing love to come into our lives can we escape pain and loneliness. It may be a romantic love, a love of children, a love of animals, or a love of friends and neighbors. We must also remember to love ourselves.

Love is within all of us. When we truly open our hearts to God, we will be free to share our love with others. If we enter into a relationship before we are spiritually ready, the relationship will never be successful. Surrender your thoughts to God and bring love into your life. Look within you and look around you. Where you see love, you see the hand of God.

Don't let yourself be misled by thinking that you can be a spiritual person and walk the spiritual road by simply praying or meditating. It can't be done. You must act on your spirituality. You must *do* something. Who do you think is really closer to God—a monk who never leaves the monastery or Mother Teresa who worked in the slums of Calcutta to alleviate hunger and suffering?

Every person has a spirit. The spirit is the part of the person that is eternal. Creator gives us our spirit; therefore, our spirit is perfect. We must try to match our actions to the spiritual part of our being. Before we can change our relationships, our communities, and the world, we must first change ourselves.

Our actions are what make our lives positive or negative. I have talked to people who have attended church or read a religious book and have claimed that the experience made them feel good. The time might have been better spent making *someone else* feel good.

Expecting to change by simply reading a book or going to church is like putting a bandage over a cancerous growth and expecting it to heal. Healing and change must come from within. The best way to begin to make change is to include God in every facet of your life.

Many people proclaim to believe in God but do not intimately include Him in their lives. God will work through you and direct your life, but only if your heart is open to His help.

Everyone has a responsibility to teach. Teaching does not mean trying to force your religious beliefs on others—it means pointing out the serious problems the world is facing and showing a person how he or she can help solve these problems. The very best way to teach is by letting your actions set an example for others to follow.

When you do talk to people, think about how you will be received. Just as Creator appears to each group of people in their own form, try to blend in with the people you are approaching. If you want to talk to a group of seniors in a retirement home and you bop in with green hair and a miniskirt, you will probably not be well-received.

You can't change people's lives overnight. Don't overwhelm them by asking them to do things they might find impossible. Start out with small suggestions that will be easy to carry out. Ask them to send a postcard, sign a petition, or give an article of clothing to a homeless shelter.

Let your spirituality push the negative forces out of your life. If, each day, you simply commit one small act of kindness, you will begin to bring positive energy into your life. That positive energy will work as a mirror and will reflect positive things back into your life. When you are in touch with your spiritual self, your daily life will take on a new direction.

Many people are really turned off by what some are calling the modern-day "holy wars." A lot of people seem to be more concerned with building church membership, and therefore church funds, than actually going out and helping others. When people come to my door *trying to convert me* to their religion, I explain to them that I follow my own religion. If they will not respect my beliefs, I simply hand them a list of groups in the community that need volunteers. I suggest that since they obviously have time to spare, they might better utilize that time by helping others. Speaking bluntly doesn't always make you popular, but it is sometimes necessary.

Some of the most hateful people I know believe they are deeply religious. Many of these individuals actually lived very productive lives before they "found religion." Now they live in a world surrounded only by their church members and believe that about 90 percent of the people on Earth are on a direct road to hell. They are very quick-tempered and seem to be under tremendous stress. It is impossible to even carry on a conversation without them trying to force their religion upon you.

When you take a closer look at the lives of some who are caught up in "religious fervor," you will find that they are suffering in a bad relationship or have experienced terrible tragedy. They may be filled with guilt brought about by bad choices they have made in the past.

A woman once told me that she had never been prejudiced until she found Jesus Christ. Now that she was a Christian, she realized that prejudice was necessary. I'm sure that Jesus would not agree with her.

On the other hand, I had a friend who claimed to be an atheist. However, she spent her whole life doing nothing but helping others. She gave and gave and gave. She became an alcoholic and then progressed into drugs. During this time, she continued to help others. One day she decided to quit, cold turkey. She did so and never fell back into addiction. She did not turn to doctors or self-help groups to accomplish this.

If you had talked to this woman once she was sober, she would have told you that she achieved sobriety by herself. I believe she attained her goal with the help of Creator. This woman, who spent her entire life sacrificing to help others, eventually died peacefully in her sleep. Although she was an atheist, she had lived an exemplary life in the service of others. I believe that when she died, she was probably very surprised to find Creator waiting to welcome her into the Spirit World.

Your salvation is not in your words or even in your thoughts. Your actions and deeds toward other humans, all living creatures, and the sacred Earth upon which we walk will one day guide your spirit on its journey to the Spirit World.

When missionaries travel to far-off lands, are they really trying to help or are they trying to convert more people to their religious beliefs? A truly spiritual person will give help without thought of reward. Be a *helper*, not a *hustler*.

Churches should not be businesses concerned only with filling their collection plates. No matter what church, synagogue, or temple we pray in, our prayers are heard by the same God. The time spent on religious disagreement and debate would be much better spent in the service of others.

Your spiritual life should not be limited to one morning a week in church. It should be part of your daily activities. The spiritual beliefs you follow should be held within your heart and be the basis for every thought, word, and deed.

Arrogance is not a spiritual quality. If you infer that your relationship with God is superior to that of someone else, you are putting yourself in the position of judge and jury. You don't know the depth of that person's relationship with God. You don't know how God views that person's life. You only know that the person's beliefs are different from your own.

We each have an obligation to seek out our own personal truth. We must push our ego aside and allow our spirit to guide us. The only thing of real value that people have is their soul or spirit. We must engage in a search to get in touch with our spirit. Only then can we bring truth and meaning to our lives.

Prayer enables us to speak with God. Prayer brings God's strength and will into our lives. Prayer opens our hearts to allow God's holy spirit to enter and guide us through each day. Through prayer, we bring God's love into our lives. We will experience rebirth through prayer.

God's love is stronger than any problem we face. Through prayer or meditation, God's healing forces will raise us above our problems. God's love is stronger than alcohol, stronger than drug addiction, and stronger than hatred. God's love is stronger than our illnesses or disabilities. You, as God's creation, are a powerful person. Release that power through prayer.

If you experience feelings of failure, you are simply disconnected from your spiritual power. Take time to pray every day. Bring God back into your life. God's love for you is endless. God was a part of your life when you were born. If you feel you have now lost communication with God, sincere prayer will bring Him back into your life.

Prayer gives us power. When we pray, our spirit is lifted. Our minds open to new and meaningful thought. Anything we have experienced in life can help us grow and improve. Through prayer we can overcome our past. We no longer have to be victims. God can heal all pain and sorrow, and give us a new life.

When you ask God for something, ask not for the gift but the strength to achieve it. Don't ask for God to give you a mate; pray for the ability to go out and find a mate. Don't ask God to make you lose ten pounds; pray for the willpower to stop eating fatty foods and the strength to exercise daily. God gave us minds and ability and we must put them to use in the best manner possible.

Many people don't pray until they are gravely ill or facing death. Prayer can change your life, heal you, and make you whole. Don't wait until you are in a desperate situation. Pray daily. Prayer is easy. Just talk to God. When you pray or meditate, you will change. Ask for God's guidance in every situation:

❖ Ask Him to remove all thoughts that are negative.

❖ Ask Him to remove hatred from your heart.

❖ Ask Him to show you the good in all people.

❖ Ask Him to give you patience when it is most needed.

❖ Ask Him to remove anger from your dealings with others.

❖ Ask Him for the gift of honesty.

❖ Ask Him for the strength to better serve His divine purpose.

❖ Ask Him to help you develop to the highest level any talents that He has given you.

❖ Ask Him to help you become the best you can possibly be.

When God shows you His wishes, you must act upon them. You must guide your children along life's pathway. You must have the strength to leave an abusive relationship. You must have the courage to do the things that are necessary in life and the willpower to stay away from things that you know are wrong. You must make the right decisions. If you know something is wrong, don't do it. Never attempt to leave something in the hands of God and do nothing. God accepts reasons, but He does not accept excuses. God will work through us, but we must *work*. Never underestimate the power of the individual. To save the human race, we must begin by saving ourselves.

It is easy to say that we can't be blamed for the wrongs of our fathers. It is true that we should not have to accept blame for their wrongdoings. However, if we see the wrongs and do nothing to correct them, we are as guilty as the person who first committed them. If you're not part of the solution, you're part of the problem.

As a creation of God, any person can become a spiritual being. It's very easy to begin. Start by making a decision to leave your past behind and look to the future. An easy way to check on your progress is to keep a small notebook at your bedside. Every night before you go to sleep, write down the good things you did that day. Did you do any volunteer work? This does not mean mailing out letters trying to convert others to your religion or attending a religious study group. This means *doing something* to actually help someone:

- ❖ Did you open a door for a person whose arms were full of packages?

- ❖ Did you slow down to allow a car to change lanes on the freeway?

- ❖ Did you do anything to make a stranger's life easier?

❖ Did you place a pan of water in a shady place so that birds and creatures passing through your yard might be able to drink on a hot day?

❖ Did you do something to protect a wild creature?

❖ Did you do anything to help heal the Earth?

As you build a closer relationship with God, the pages of your notebook will fill up faster and faster. As your notebook pages fill, your life will also fill with joy and peace. When you awaken each morning, think about some of the positive things you would like to do that day.

A helpful exercise is to get some index cards and on one side of the card write down a word that describes any negative thought you have or act you commit. For instance, if you find yourself not wanting to share with someone, write "selfish" on one side of the card. Almost every negative has a positive. So, if you write "selfish" on one side of the card, on the other side write "generous." Every night before going to bed and every morning upon arising, read only the positive side of the cards. Focus on the positive. Kindness, honesty, responsibility, acceptance, love, sacrifice, generosity—these words will soon describe your actions.

I remember a day, quite a few years ago, when my Salvadoran gardener, Manuel, taught me a lesson in compassion. We were driving down Wilshire Boulevard in Los Angeles. Standing on a corner, waving his arms in the air and yelling, was a man everyone calls "Old Frank." It was obvious that the man had not bathed for many months. His blackened skin was cracked and bloody; raw patches were visible. His long hair and beard were matted. Worn shoes covered his dirty feet. A newspaper was crammed into the crotch of his filthy trousers to cover the open area extending from knee to knee where his pants had simply rotted away.

Even though we were enclosed in the safety of my car, I shuddered as we drove past him. Making a face I uttered, "Oh, my God!"

Manuel looked at the unfortunate man on the street corner. With a sad face, he quietly said, "Oh, the poor man."

I felt terrible. Riding in the luxury of my expensive new car, I had failed to feel compassion for one who obviously was in great need. I prayed for forgiveness and vowed never to let anything like that happen again. Later that week I packed some boxes with food and took them to a homeless shelter. In a city as large as Los Angeles, it is safer to work with the shelters than to try to approach anyone on the street. You want to help people, but you also want to live to be able to continue to give.

Goodness and kindness should become a way of life. We must *live* in a spiritual manner. In traditional Native American life, everything is spiritual. The languages have no exact translation for the word "religion." There is no clear divide between the sacred and the secular. Religious values are a part of every day life.

Whether at home or in the workplace, be courteous in your dealings with others. When you show disrespect for another, you show disrespect for yourself. However, when you get in the habit of treating others politely, it becomes an everyday occurrence. Courtesy is contagious. Some of those who benefit from your kind behavior will begin to act the same way toward others. It will continue to spread. This is a very small step toward world peace, but it is a step.

You need only turn on the evening news or pick up a newspaper to be reminded of the violence in our society. There is no reason for one person to ever strike another. This does not mean you cannot defend yourself, but don't be the one to strike the first blow. It's all right to fight back if you are mugged, but it's not all right to go out and mug someone.

Try to spread the power of God's love through every act you commit. Before it was politically incorrect to call a woman a lady, my grandmother used to say, "The first quality of a lady is kindness." I have always believed that. If someone asks me what I find most attractive in a man, I will always answer "kindness." If every person would be completely kind, all the world's problems would be solved.

Spirituality is not a state of mind; it is a state of continuous action. When your mind is truly in the right place, you cannot help but act on your positive thoughts. There can be no separation between spirituality and life. It is not what you *believe* or *say* that matters—it is what you *do*.

When you act in a truly spiritual manner, you help others as well as improve your own life. God did not put us on Earth to be miserable. He does not want us to be unhappy. When we become spiritually sound, we will also bring emotional, physical, and economic soundness into our lives.

Spiritual soundness leads to success. When your success is achieved through honest effort you have earned your rewards. Success is measured differently by each person trying to achieve it. A physically challenged athlete running a marathon is a success. An actor who wins an Oscar is a success. We all have different goals and when we reach them, we are successful. There is nothing wrong with reaching goals, whether financial or emotional, as long as they are not achieved at the expense of another person.

Poverty does not necessarily bring us closer to God. The belief that the meek shall inherit the Earth is a politically convenient statement. If a wealthy person can keep his workers laboring for less than minimum wage, with a promise of reward in the afterlife, he will only become wealthier and his workers will only sink deeper into poverty.

Physical health brings value to our lives. We should respect the life that God has given us. We do not act in a spiritual manner when we abuse our bodies with drugs, excessive alcohol, or tobacco used for something other than ceremonial purposes. Our body is the temple God created to house our spirit. We should not abuse that which God has created.

There are many positive things we can do that are not only simple, but also very enjoyable. Make a list and choose to do the things you would enjoy the most. Talk to friends and relatives about what you are doing. You don't necessarily need to mention that you are trying to improve your spiritual life. You can simply tell them that what you are doing is necessary and also fun. You might then suggest that they do something similar. The list of possibilities is endless. Here are a few suggestions:

❖ Don't buy any woods (furniture, etc.) that come from rainforests. Boycott stores that sell them and make the store manager or owner aware of the boycott.

❖ Volunteer to make audio tapes for the visually impaired.

❖ Take animals on visits to senior citizen homes.

❖ Clean up the side of a roadway.

❖ Be a Big Sister or Big Brother.

❖ Be a hospital candy striper.

❖ Write letters or postcards to save endangered species, the environment, etc.

❖ Take a bag of food to a homeless shelter.

❖ Volunteer to help with a charity.

When you begin to do these things, even though you do them selflessly, your rewards will still be great. You will make new friends, your social life will improve, you might acquire business contacts, and you may even find new, more meaningful employment. Because you have helped others, your spirit will soar.

Only today is important. Yesterday is gone—you cannot change it. You have not yet lived tomorrow. Today is the only time you have to make changes. To truly walk the sacred path, you must live each day to the best of your ability.

In this troubled world, peace is still possible. Peace will begin with only one person. The world will be healed, one small step at a time. If every person simply does his or her small part, the Earth will be saved.

CHAPTER TWENTY

After My Return

*I ask you in the name of justice for repose, for
myself and my injured people . . . that
another outrage may never be committed . . .
and when the hand of oppression is stretched
against us, let me hope that every part of the
United States, filling the mountains and
valleys, will echo and say stop . . .*

—George Harkins, District Chief,
Choctaw Nation, 1832

*B*eing in a hospital or bedridden for a long period of
time is a very humbling experience. The first time I was back
in a car, everything looked so new. I felt a sense of surprise
that the world had continued as if nothing unusual had
happened. My life had almost stopped—it seemed that
everything else should have stopped also. But that didn't
happen. Everything and everyone went right on as if I had
never lived at all. I felt like yelling, "Hey, stop! Don't you
know what happened to me? Aren't you glad to see me back

again?" But, of course, no one even noticed me. I felt as if I were invisible.

The suffering I endured while in that county hospital was extraordinary. Other than the initial surgery, I received little care. The doctors didn't even wire my broken jaw until I had been in the hospital three days. I'm sure they assumed I was going to die so they didn't want to waste any more time on me.

I was not given anything to eat or drink. Only if I was conscious and able to ask a nurse or patient passing by my bed for water, did I receive any liquid. I had no food. I was not catheterized, and once or twice a day I had to ask another patient to help me into the bathroom. If that wasn't enough to worry about, the few times that I was able to think clearly, I was concerned that I would be fired from my job at the bar for missing so much work.

During one of the times I was conscious I opened my eyes to see Rick, my employer from the bar, standing at the foot of my bed. Rick and I detested each other and I sincerely doubted that he cared if I lived or died.

"Oh my God, I've died again and there really is a hell," I groaned. I considered this a real possibility. I closed my eyes hoping that this apparition would disappear, but when I opened them again, Rick was still standing there, looking very frightened. I decided he must have come to make peace with me before I died and came back to haunt him.

"What are you doing here?" I managed to ask.

Rick told me how concerned he was and assured me that he would hold my job open for as long as necessary. He said that he and his wife, Marilyn, would be happy to keep Pete for me until I was well. I thanked him, but said that Pete was well cared for by Buena, our live-in babysitter.

The next day, Jim came to the hospital with his sister, Dee, and her friend, Joanne. He told me not to worry about Pete because he was taking care of him. He explained that he had called my apartment, learned of my accident and immediately drove down from Idyllwild to get Pete. He had taken him back up to the mountains where they went fishing and camping, all the while trying to convince Pete that I would soon be well. Pete and Jim were together, just as I had seen from the Spirit World.

My grandparents drove to the hospital from Orange County a couple of times. They were, of course, worried but they were neither physically nor financially able to be of any help. I felt very guilty that I was causing them such anxiety.

Each day I became a little stronger, but I was still slightly delirious. The hospital had no air conditioning and the room I was in was very hot and stuffy. To try to escape from the heat, I took off my hospital gown and wrapped myself in just a bed sheet.

One day I found a dime and I began to use it to reach the operator and make collect phone calls. I walked down the hall to the pay phone wearing nothing but a bedsheet. I had to walk past two men who were handcuffed to their beds. I guess they were inmates from the Los Angeles County jail. I'm sure I looked so terrible that the men wouldn't have noticed whether I wore a sheet or not.

My friend, Mike, and my neighbor, Barbara, said I used to call them collect day and night. I would even call one of them at three or four in the morning and tell them the doctors were releasing me. They would drive over to get me, but of course it was always a false alarm. Since Mike and Barbara were not relatives, they couldn't have me transferred to a better hospital.

One day, after the operator put through a collect call for me, my dime was not returned. I felt I had lost my lifeline to the outside world.

Fortunately, I soon became strong enough to sign myself out. When I returned home from the hospital, I barely weighed ninety pounds. A friend called a county worker who came to my apartment and placed me on Medi-Cal to take care of my medical expenses. My neighbor's father was a vascular surgeon and he arranged for me to be seen by one of his associates who immediately admitted me to Cedars of Lebanon Hospital where I remained for ten days.

A few days before I was to be released from Cedars, Jim brought Pete back to Buena so he would be there when I came home. I later learned that Pete had spent most evenings downstairs with Mary and her niece, Helen. They were very fond of Pete and did their best to assure him that I would be home soon. Mary told me that one night they were playing a game where the winner got to make a wish. When Pete won, he said, "I wish my mother would live." Mary admitted that it was all she and Helen could do to keep from crying. I still feel pain when I think of the fear my young son must have experienced, thinking that his mother might be taken from him.

When I was once again home from the hospital, I realized that, until I could return to work, money would be very tight. Even though it was not yet fall, I began to worry about Christmas. Pete always looked forward to the holidays; no matter how broke I was I always managed to have a beautiful tree with lots of presents under it for him.

Pete and I always bought our tree from the tree lots by the train yards. We would go after midnight, when only one or two men were working guarding the lots. They always felt sorry for a young woman alone with a child and gave us very good prices on trees.

When we tied the tree onto the top of the car we would then have to climb in through the windows because the doors were held shut by the rope. The rope we used was a very thick, white silky rope that had been used to hold crowds back at the premier of the Beatles' movie, *The Yellow Submarine.* I had been a guest at the premier and after it was over someone had given me the rope as a souvenir. It quickly became our official "Christmas tree rope."

Having a big Christmas and new school clothes for Pete each September seemed to be my most important financial responsibilities. No matter what the sacrifice, those two things were paramount. I knew I could manage to buy school clothes, but I was afraid that this would be Pete's first Christmas with few or no presents.

When I explained to Pete that this might be a very small Christmas, he looked at me and said very seriously, "Mom, you're alive and that's the best Christmas present I could ever have." He was only eight years old.

As it turned out we enjoyed a marvelous holiday season. Shortly before Christmas, I managed to get on a television game show and won. Fortunately, my prizes included many wonderful gifts for Pete.

I believe I definitely am a survivor. Even when things appear to be hopeless, I somehow always manage to pull through. I also believe I have strong Spirit Protectors watching over me.

Nonetheless, our financial situation was not good. When you are very young, it is hard to believe that terrible things can happen. I never even thought about having medical insurance. I learned a hard lesson. After my accident, I made certain that Pete and I were always adequately insured.

As soon as I began to get my strength back, I could think of nothing but getting back to Mexico. To say that I was obsessed with a certain young man below the border was an understatement. Even though I was in tremendous pain, nothing could keep me from traveling back to Tijuana and the handsome, young bullfighter.

I went to Tijuana every time Francisco was in from Mexico City, but something had changed. I still loved being in Mexico, but now my time in Tijuana was spent only with Francisco. Friends asked me to go to nightclubs with them, but I refused. Everywhere I looked, I saw something wrong with our modern society. I saw greed, jealousy, hatred, prejudice, and a total lack of caring for other human beings. I, of course, had been aware of these things in the past, but it seemed like I had viewed them through a thin veil. Now it was as if the veil had been lifted and my vision had been sharpened. When I saw all of these things, I felt great pain and sadness.

Since my journey to the Spirit World, I knew many things I had not known before. Actually, I probably had known them, but they must have been buried deep within my subconscious. I realized I had to make others aware of the changes we must make. I understood that the problems were so great that if we did not begin to do something immediately, the world as we know it would end. I began to talk to everyone about things we could do to save ourselves, our societies, and our Earth. I wanted to tell everyone that I had died, traveled to the Spirit World, and been shown the total destruction that our current lifestyles would bring about. However, I knew if I said I had returned from the dead, people would think that I was crazy.

I continued to talk constantly about the problems facing society. Even my conversations with Francisco took on a new tone. Our conversations were never easy. He spoke some English, I spoke some Spanish, and we both spoke a little French. If I called him at his home in Mexico City, I had to use a girlfriend of mine who spoke fluent Spanish to translate.

I felt frustrated that I could not more adequately express my thoughts. The few things I was able to relate, Francisco responded to with care and understanding. Although his father was also a bullfighter and he had grown up in a wealthy and privileged family, for such a young man he was capable of great degrees of kindness and concern. He had a great sense of honor, honesty, and caring for those around him and the world at large. There was none of the spoiled superstar persona that was so obvious in some of his peers.

Francisco and I continued to see each other for another year. During the winter while he was fighting in Mexico City, he was offered a two-year contract in Spain. Before he left, he resumed his romance with and married his childhood sweetheart. At about the same time, I became seriously involved with a young Native American man whom I met at one of my political functions.

Since then, whenever Francisco and I happen to meet, we still enjoy seeing each other. I find him the same kind, wonderful person he always was. I have great memories of the time we spent together.

In the fall of 1969, I went to UCLA to attend a lecture. I was wandering through the halls, late and lost, when I saw a tall young Native American man approaching. I asked if he could give me directions to the lecture. He said he was also looking for the room, so I walked along with him. When we reached the lecture, it had already begun so we entered quietly and sat at the back of the room. During the break, we introduced ourselves. He was Richard Oakes from the Mohawk Nation in upper state New York. He, his wife Annie, and their children were now living in San Francisco. Richard explained that he and a group of other Native Americans were planning to reclaim Alcatraz Island as native land. (Native Americans have long said that when the buffalo return, it will be from the west. Alcatraz is as far west as you can go, so this was a very symbolic gesture.)

I agreed to join Richard and the others. In my little blue Volkswagen, I followed a caravan of UCLA students to San Francisco. In the dark, damp San Francisco Bay, we had boats waiting that would transport us, without using any lights, to the tiny island with its history of violence and suffering.

With the first rays of dawn's light, we gathered in a circle to hold a meeting. We debated just how far we should take our stand. Should we simply make a statement by staying 24 hours and then leave? Should we stay longer and risk arrest or even death at the hands of a trigger-happy government agent? The UCLA students were worried about missing their classes and even more worried about the UCLA vans they had left parked on the mainland. They had been given permission to take the vans to attend a conference in San Francisco. The university certainly would not be happy to learn that its vans had transported students to take over a piece of government land.

When it was my turn to speak, I spoke out strongly. I said that we had already come this far and our relatives who had lived before us were depending on us to act with courage and honor. This was our land and we should not allow anyone to remove us. Everyone agreed and suddenly no one wanted to leave. The reaction of the group was so strong that I realized that the words I had spoken had not been my own. Creator had given those words to me.

That first morning we were a very small group, but soon we were joined by many others. Our first few hours on the island were very meaningful. There was a caretaker who was understandably frightened and stayed pretty much to himself. For the first time in more than a century, we were under no laws but our own. We were once again independent nations and could do exactly as we pleased. Though we were still new and struggling to regain our traditions that had long ago been taken from us, we felt for the first time in our lives that we were truly and completely free.

I stayed on Alcatraz as long as I could before having to go back to work to pay rent and provide food for Pete who was now being cared for by a girlfriend staying at my apartment. I continued to return to the island as often as I could, even taking Pete with me when I felt it was safe. While I was working in Los Angeles, I collected food for the people still staying on Alcatraz and also spoke at many public meetings as well as on radio and television to raise support for the struggle.

When I traveled back to the island shortly before Christmas, I learned that both the group's money and food supply were almost gone. I volunteered to help raise the needed cash.

Two weeks after I returned to Los Angeles, I was able to put together a major concert with several top rock groups including Eric Burdon & War, The Byrds, Delaney & Bonnie and Friends, Geronimo Black from Frank Zappa's Mothers of Invention, and Cream's drummer, Ginger Baker. Jim Morrison of the Doors had promised to be Master of Ceremonies, but at the last minute was unable to make it. I ended up hosting the show.

The music world was in shock. Everyone wanted to know who had put together this important musical event. When they learned that it was a Choctaw woman from Alcatraz who had no experience in the music world whatsoever and that she had done it in only two weeks, the shock was even greater. It was common consensus that putting together a show like this in two weeks was something of a miracle. And it was.

My recruitment methods for the concert had been unorthodox, to say the least. I had managed to get upstairs into one of the dressing rooms at Hollywood's Whisky a Go Go to talk to one of the groups. I found Eric Burdon in the bar at The Troubadour, where he had been appearing. This is definitely not the usual way to approach superstars, but it worked. When the concert ended successfully and I was preparing to return to Alcatraz, I took a moment to reflect upon what had really happened. Looking back, I realized that I was not the one who had put this incredible concert together. My hands had done the work, but they were being guided by a much higher source. Creator had shown me the way to bring food to a group of people struggling to be free.

By the time I left Alcatraz again, my feet were firmly planted on the sacred Red Road, the spiritual path for Native Americans. For the five years before my accident, I had actively worked for Native American causes, but the commitment now became deeper.

Always in my mind was the picture of the desolate Earth I had seen when I visited the Spirit World. I knew I had to do everything I could to keep that picture from becoming a reality. Creator had clearly shown me what our future on Earth would be if we did not change our manner of living.

I felt a tremendous responsibility to warn everyone I could of the impending disaster. I had to make people understand that we need to work together. We must stop pollution and the destruction of the land. We have to put an end to the threat of nuclear war. I knew that time was running out and I feared for everyone on the planet.

My life became one of constant political activity—which led to continuous harassment by the FBI. Local police followed me and I was under constant surveillance. I was arrested twice. The first time I was released after they said it was a case of mistaken identity. The second time they told me I owed a two-dollar parking ticket. The bail would be five dollars. I didn't have any money with me, so they handcuffed my wrists and threw me in the back of the squad car. When we reached the police station, I was escorted into a back room and handcuffed to a chair. They put a blinding light in my face and began questioning me about my political activities. I really had nothing to tell them. All I had been doing in recent months was collecting food and clothes for needy families. Obviously, they thought that was criminal activity. As I sat on the hard metal chair, an older policeman walked by the open doorway. When he saw me he stopped, rattled off my address, and asked if I was living at the same place. Later, as I was still handcuffed to that stupid chair, a young policeman came by. (He obviously was new to the department because he still knew how to be polite and friendly.) He asked what I had done. I told him I had already paid the parking ticket, but his department said I had not. He asked how much the ticket was. When I told him it was two dollars, he looked astonished. He shook his head. "Someone must really be out to get you," he said apologetically. No kidding.

Then a policeman I had not seen before came into the room. He was wearing rubber gloves and he unlocked and removed my handcuffs. I thought I was going to be released, but he told me I was only being allowed to make one phone call. I immediately called a friend who said he would be right down with five dollars for my bail.

Then the policeman took me by the arm and led me to a cell. I asked why he was wearing gloves. He glared at me. "Germs," was all he said. (I'm not sure what he meant since this was years before anyone had heard of AIDS.)

He then locked me in the cell and left. I must have been in the drunk tank because the floor of the cell was covered with dried vomit. I started to feel sick. I climbed up and stood on the bench waiting for my friend to arrive.

After almost an hour, I became so angry that I decided to sing. I knew that anyone having to listen to my singing would suffer greatly. I sang every song about prisons I knew. Very quickly the same policeman returned, took me out of the cell and up to the front desk. He was still wearing rubber gloves.

I was relieved to see my friend waiting to drive me back to my car. When we left the jail he told me that he arrived and paid my bail within five or ten minutes after I had called him; the rest of the time he was waiting for me to be released. The jail was not busy, so I knew the long wait was just further harassment. I said a prayer of thanks for my terrible singing voice and made a vow to work harder to make this a country with "justice for all."

I went from one public speaking engagement to another. I coordinated media coverage when Native Americans chained themselves inside the Southwest Museum in Los Angeles to protest the museum's Native American burial displays. I was co-founder of the first chapter of the American Indian Movement in Los Angeles. I was co-founder and chairperson of United People for Wounded Knee—a coalition of groups working in support of the Native American takeover of Wounded Knee in 1973. Our group organized fundraisers, rallys, speaking tours, and publicity in Southern California for those at Wounded Knee. I was a delegate for Native American issues at the 1975 World Congress in the German Democratic Republic. As a member of the American Indian Movement, I was a plaintiff in its case against the Los Angeles Police Department for its illegal infiltration and spying tactics. The case was settled out of court for more than $1 million in favor of the American Indian Movement and other organizations.

In recent years, the main focus of my work has been directed toward the protection of children, animals, and the environment. Everywhere I speak, no matter what the topic, I always include specific things everyone can do to save our Earth.

My husband Rupert and I are very busy with our seven-year-old son, Na Humma. We do our best to instill in him traditional values and a strong respect for our sacred Mother Earth.

When our baby was born we gave him a Choctaw name that literally means "The Red One." However, a clearer translation would be "Red Warrior." The "Na Humma" may not run or turn back on the field of battle. It is a strong name that we believe he will live up to.

Na Humma's birth was a beautiful experience. Rupert was beside me the entire time and was even allowed to stay in the room with Na Humma and me the five days I was in the hospital. Cedars-Sinai in Los Angeles is an excellent hospital. I wish I could have been there when I gave birth to Pete.

Before Na Humma was one month old we took him to Rupert's reservation, the Tohono O'odham Nation in southern Arizona, for a purification ceremony performed by a medicine woman. The ceremony protects a baby and creates a bond and respect for the Earth.

We travel back and forth to the reservation as often as possible and have picked out the land near Rupert's mother's house where we will one day build a home. We are the only ones in Rupert's family who now live off the reservation.

My husband was born and raised on his reservation, and did not learn English until he was forced to attend a boarding school when he was six years old. Like many other Native American children who have attended boarding schools, Rupert's years away from home were not pleasant ones.

His school experience changed when he attended high school at Phoenix Indian School, where he joined the wrestling team. He received many awards and, in his junior year, won the state championship. This victory resulted in such a sense of pride among the students that it spurred on the other sports teams to be successful. He continued to participate in wrestling and other sports while attending college.

After we were married, Rupert began wrestling again. He competed in Canada in 1990 at the North American Indigenous Games and returned with a silver medal. He competed again in 1993 and came back with the gold. He has also begun to study judo.

Rupert loves working with children, and before we were married he coached the Little League team on his reservation. In July 1995, he plans to take several teams of young people from Arizona to participate in the North American Indigenous Games in Minneapolis.

To raise money for the teams to attend the games, Rupert has organized benefits and other fundraising efforts in Arizona. Rupert and Na Humma have also become storytellers, acting out traditional Native American stories for both small and large groups.

Rupert, Na Humma, and I also speak at elementary schools, teaching young people about Native American culture and protection of the environment. My husband and I are also writing and illustrating a series of children's books about Native American children.

Na Humma enjoys speaking and performing and well understands the environmental dangers we face today. He is very proud of his culture and participates in traditional Native American dancing as well as karate and judo.

Thankfully, my older son, Pete, still lives close enough to us that we are able to see or talk with him quite often. Besides having a black belt in judo, in the past few years he has become quite interested in roller-skating. He started out playing roller hockey with friends and then tried out for a team with the Roller Games. He made the team, whose games were televised weekly. Last year, he skated with an American team against Japanese skaters in the Tokyo Dome in Japan. When the old Roller Derby games were started up again, he signed with the L.A. Aztecs. He is considering going back to school for a higher degree in the medical field. I give thanks everyday that, although he was raised in a large city, he never had the problems with drugs or alcohol that plague so many young people today. I am very proud of my son.

I have always believed strongly in the value of family unity and was fortunate to marry a man who has the same values. A strong family raises strong children. Whatever Rupert and I do, our family always comes first. Our future and our world will one day be entrusted to our children. In the Spirit World, I was shown that our children must be prepared to handle great responsibility.

Pete grew up knowing I had died and returned to Earth. Na Humma is now beginning to learn about my experience. Rupert, being of traditional Native American thought, fully understands my journey to the Spirit World.

My life and rebirth at such an early age have given our family a deeper appreciation of life. We accept the fragility of life on Earth while understanding that life is eternal. This knowledge encourages us to live each day to the fullest and yet have no fears about life in the next world. It has provided us with a sense of spiritual peace, but has also created an urgency to do everything in our power to carry out the instructions shown to me by Creator.

We are at a precarious time in the history of our world. We must put our greed and jealousies aside and work together to save our civilization and the planet. No one person can do it alone, yet no government can make the needed changes without each individual doing his or her part. Only the love we give and the good deeds we perform during our lifetime have any real meaning. All else is illusion. What we do while on Earth prepares our spirit for eternity. Our life on Earth is very short and none of us can escape our final destiny.

We are here because Creator has given us the gift of life. We must understand our mission and willingly put ourselves into His service. If we sincerely try, with Creator's help, we will succeed.